EMERSON

A Statement of
New England Transcendentalism
as Expressed in the Philosophy of
Its Chief Exponent

BY

HENRY DAVID GRAY

FREDERICK UNGAR PUBLISHING CO.
NEW YORK

Third Printing, 1970

Printed in the United States of America

ISBN 0-8044-1305-3

Library of Congress Catalog Card No. 58-9333

CONTENTS

PREFACE

This thesis was completed just at the time when Emerson's Journals were announced for publication. Thus it happened that the writer had either to print an essay which was antiquated in advance, or wait until the Journals could be read and the book revised in accordance with the "new evidence." The delay of publication—prolonged beyond all expectation—was granted by the Columbia Faculty of Philosophy, and at the same time permission was given to add chapters on Emerson's contribution to ethics, sociology, and esthetics, in order that a certain completeness might be given to the subject. The Journals continued to appear at intervals until 1914. No revision of the original thesis has been made necessary by them, but they have gone far to confirm the attitude which was taken at the start; for the whole purport of this study was to trace the development of Emerson's thought and to find how far the ideas to which he gives a fragmentary and poetic rendering are consistent parts of a larger theory. It has always been known that it was Emerson's custom to make use in his essays and addresses of ideas which he had jotted down in his note-books years before; the publication of these note-books reveals just how and when the idea first came into his mind. But inasmuch as these ideas have received a more perfect expression in the essays and addresses, it has seldom been found necessary or advisable to quote from them; and since there has been little of importance concerning Emerson's philosophy published since 1904, the essay as now set forth stands practically as it originally did through Chapter VII. References to the Journals here and there, as well as to Mr. Goddard's *Studies in New England Transcendentalism,* Mr. Firkins' *Ralph Waldo Emerson,* and Professor Woodbridge Riley's *American Thought,* with some other contributions to the subject made since this essay was first written, have been added without changing more than the immediate context.

References to the works of Emerson are to the paging of the Riverside edition, since the thesis was written before the Centenary edition was completed; but the notes of Dr. Edward Waldo Emerson, as well as the additional matter included in the later edition, have been read in connection with the Journals for this revision of the essay.

After so many years I still remember with gratitude the friendly assistance given me by Professor Frederick J. E. Woodbridge, under whose direction the thesis was prepared; that it has so many rhetorical as well as philosophical shortcomings is due largely to the fact that it had to be written for the most part without his personal guidance. My thanks are due also to Professor Warner Fite of Indiana University, to Professor Killis Campbell of the University of Texas, to Professor John Erskine of Columbia University, and to Professor H. W. Stuart of Leland Stanford Junior University, for friendly criticisms and suggestions. There are, as always, other obligations not the less appreciated because not publicly acknowledged.

H. D. G.

STANFORD UNIVERSITY, May 1917.

EMERSON

A STATEMENT OF NEW ENGLAND TRANSCENDENTALISM
AS EXPRESSED IN THE PHILOSOPHY OF
ITS CHIEF EXPONENT

INTRODUCTION

The term "New England Transcendentalism" is applied, first, to the various phases of idealism which found expression in New England during, roughly, the second quarter of the nineteenth century. But an examination of the attitude of that group of men who are recognized as the New England Transcendentalists soon reveals the fact that they themselves were not primarily concerned with philosophy for its own sake, but imported and modified the thought of Plato, of the Neo-Platonists and Mystics, or of Kant and his successors, merely as a basis for their attitude toward religion and conduct; that they thought of Transcendentalism not only as a philosophy but as a "movement"; that however they might differ in theory, they were Transcendentalists by virtue of a common impulse. "This spirit of the time," says Emerson in his manifesto in the opening number of *The Dial*, "is in every form a protest against usage, and a search for principles."[1] This is a second meaning of the term "New England Transcendentalism." A third meaning, which has been the source of much confusion, may be summed up in the phrase "Transcendental nonsense." The Transcendental movement was attended by a general spirit of unrest and hostility to convention. Whims and absurdities of all sorts were in the air. "Bran had its prophets, and the presartorial simplicity of Adam its martyrs," writes Lowell, in his delightful essay on Thoreau. "Everybody had a mission (with a capital M) to attend to everybody else's business. No brain but had its private maggot, which must have found pitiably short commons sometimes." And in the same spirit Hawthorne, in his *American Note-Books,* speaks of Margaret Fuller's refractory cow at Brook Farm as a "transcendental heifer." The name New England Transcendentalism has been applied to cover all the wild vagaries of the time.

---

[1] "The Editors to the Reader," *Dial,* I, 3.

There was some excuse for this. The first announcements of Transcendentalism [2] were incomprehensible, and hence an immediate source of mirth, to "ordinary" and "sensible" people; an abstruseness of utterance was so often combined with eccentricity of conduct that it was easy to laugh at both of them together.[3] Even the scholarly and the learned were bewildered by the first writings of Emerson [4] and Alcott; and of the latter, at least, the absurd side, both in the "Orphic Sayings" and in the Fruitlands venture, is still quite apparent. "I was given to understand," says Dickens in his *American Notes,* "that whatever was unintelligible would be certainly Transcendental." [5] "Transcendentalism" was the name applied to whatever lay beyond the realm of common sense, whether in thought, language, or behavior.[6]

The connection between the half-mad representatives of what they called "The Newness" and the more serious exponents of Transcendentalism proper was so close that it is hard to know where to draw the line. Emerson himself, the most conspicuously sane man among them all, was thought mad in the first extreme expression of his individualism, and the most foolish of his associates had, or thought he had, his own peculiar variation of the "intuitional philosophy." It is impossible to set up some arbitrary standard of sense and sanity, and say that whoever fell below this standard was *not* a transcendentalist. It is better to admit frankly that all three meanings of the term are quite legitimate provided that no one meaning is used to the exclusion of the other two; that New England Transcendentalism had its philosophic side, which in Emerson

---

[2] I use the word always as referring to New England Transcendentalism.

[3] As, for example, in such a man as Charles Newcomb, not to mention others. One need not be a philistine for failing to take such a man with perfect sobriety. "Emerson was convinced that Newcomb's remarkable subtlety of mind amounted to genius," says Lindsay Swift (*Brook Farm,* p. 199), and proceeds to quote a sentence from "Dolon," which appeared in *The Dial,* as showing "if not genius, its next of kin." Newcomb's absurdities of conduct were also famous.

[4] Holmes compares Professor Francis Bowen reviewing Emerson's *Nature,* to "a sagacious pointer making the acquaintance of a box tortoise." There is more than humor in this; yet Bowen showed more comprehension of Transcendentalism than any other critic on the "outside."

[5] The members of the group were of course conscious of their reputation. "I should have told them at once that I was a transcendentalist," says Thoreau. "That would have been the shortest way of telling them that they would not understand my explanations." *Journal,* V, 4.

[6] Emerson breaks into delicious raillery when speaking of the whims and oddities of some of his associates; while two such good transcendentalists as James Freeman Clarke and C. P. Cranch illustrated Emerson himself with humorous drawings for their own amusement. See G. W. Cooke, "Contributors to *The Dial*," *Journal of Speculative Philosophy,* XIX, 236.

at least found a worthy and noble expression; that primarily it was a movement in religion, literature, and conduct; and that its camp followers were disproportionately numerous and noisy.

Though the distinction between the philosophical and practical sides of New England Transcendentalism was made by Noah Porter as early as 1842,[7] this distinction was never recognized by its adherents, and has seldom been taken into account by its critics. We find Transcendentalism described now as a philosophy,[8] now as an expression of religious faith,[9] and again as a wave of reform.[10] Frothingham, who has written the history of the movement from the standpoint of a sympathizer and former adherent, defines Transcendentalism from all three points of view without making the least distinction in his use of the term: "Transcendentalism was a distinct philosophical system. Practically it was an assertion of the inalienable worth of man; theoretically it was an assertion of the immanence of divinity in instinct, the transference of supernatural attributes to the natural constitution of mankind." Again, "Transcendentalism is usually spoken of as a philosophy. It is more justly regarded as a gospel. As a philosophy it is . . . so far from uniform in its structure, that it may rather be considered several systems than one." And yet again, "Transcendentalism was . . . an enthusiasm, a wave of sentiment, a breath of mind."[11]

But even the sum of all these views of Transcendentalism does not exhaust its content. A philosophy, a gospel, a wave of sentiment,— Transcendentalism was also a challenge. "The problem of transcendental philosophy," says Theodore Parker, "is no less than this, to revise the experience of mankind and try its teachings by the nature of man-

---

[7] "The word Transcendentalism, as used at the present day, has two applications, one of which is popular and indefinite, the other, philosophical and precise. In the former sense it describes men, rather than opinions, since it is freely extended to those who hold opinions, not only diverse from each other, but directly opposed." *Bib. Repos.,* Second Series, VIII, 195.

[8] "Transcendentalism . . . is the recognition in man of the capacity of knowing truth intuitively, or of attaining a scientific knowledge of an order of existence *transcending* the reach of the senses, and of which we can have no sensible experience." *Dial,* II, 90. Attributed by Cooke to J. A. Saxton.

[9] Literally, a passing beyond all media in the approach to the Deity, Transcendentalism contained an effort to establish, mainly by a discipline of the intuitive faculty, direct intercourse between the soul and God." Charles J. Woodbury: *Talks with Ralph Waldo Emerson,* p. 110.

[10] Transcendentalism was not . . . speculative, but essentially practical and reformatory." John Orr: "The Transcendentalism of New England." *Internat. R.,* XIII, 390.

[11] *Transcendentalism in New England,* pp. 136, 302, and 355.

kind; to test ethics by conscience, science by reason; to try the creeds
of the churches, the constitutions of the states, by the constitution of the
universe." [12]   It was because they felt that the "intuitional philosophy"
gave them full warrant for such extravangant claims that the adherents
of Transcendentalism so eagerly embraced it.   As a challenge it was received by its opponents; and because so many on each side were clergy-
men, much of the earlier discussion of Transcendentalism took the form
of religious controversy.   Thus to Emerson's Divinity School address
Andrews Norton answered with his "Latest Form of Infidelity," and to
this again Ripley replied.   *The Dial* set forth the claims of Transcendentalism as an outgrowth of Unitarianism and at the same time an attack
upon its fundamental principles,[13] while the *Princeton Review* and the
Christian Examiner alike warned their readers against it.[14]   The Unitarians opposed the new movement with especial persistence because here
it was internal dissension and civil war.

But it was mere blindness in the Unitarians not to see that Transcendentalism and the abolishment of creed were inherent in the very
creed to which they clung.   Unitarianism was essentially an assertion of
the divinity of human nature, and hence of the ability of the soul to recognize religious truths independently of authority.   But in maintaining
this the Unitarians felt themselves to be true adherents of the church.
They felt that the Protestant church was founded on the right of private judgment as superior to ecclesiastical tradition; that Christianity,
Protestantism, and Unitarianism were successive revolts proceeding from
exactly the same principle, each group of "come-outers" having the same
noble heresy that had been the corner-stone of the church from which

---

[12] Lecture on Transcendentalism.   *Works,* Centenary Edition, VI, 37.

[13] "This movement grew out of the Unitarian movement.   It did not, however, grow out of the Unitarian theology. . . . The association is, philosophically
speaking, purely accidental."   *Dial,* I, 421.   Attributed by Cooke to W. D. Wilson.
The tone of the article is openly hostile to the current orthodox Unitarianism.

[14] "We feel it to be a solemn duty to warn our readers, and in our measure,
the public, against this German atheism, which the spirit of darkness is employing
ministers of the gospel to smuggle in among us under false pretenses."   *Princeton
Review,* XII, 71.   By Charles Hodge, the "founder, editor, and principal contrib-
utor."   (See Index Volume.)   The *Princeton Review* was the orthodox Presby-
terian organ.

"We have no taste for the sublimated atheism of Fichte, or the downright
pantheism of Schelling.   Yet these are men familiar with the works of such
authors, and loud in their praise, who are not ashamed to charge the philosophy of
Locke with a sensualizing and degrading influence."   *Christian Examiner,* XXIII,
181.   By F[rancis] B[owen].   The *Christian Examiner* was the Unitarian organ,
but was already inclining toward the more liberal wing.

they withdrew before it developed a creed and an authority of its own. Channing, who led the revolt from Congregationalism, saw the love of creed and authority at work again and said sadly, "We have a Unitarian orthodoxy." From this "orthodoxy" Transcendentalism was the next revolt;[15] but although at first it took some members out of the church, in the end it triumphed within the church; and the Unitarians today are much more the followers of Emerson and Parker than of their bitter and forgotten antagonists. However much more it may have been, Transcendentalism was a development in the history of the Unitarian church.

So important is the religious aspect of Transcendentalism that one is sometimes tempted to regard it not only as fundamental but as all-inclusive. It should be remembered, however, that no history of American literature or of American social progress could be written without taking account of the Transcendental movement. But it is beyond the purpose of this essay to consider Transcendentalism from any of these points of view. Our purpose is merely to frame a working definition as a basis for a consideration of Emerson's philosophy; and it has seemed best to bring together such statements as have hitherto been made, so far as they do not merely repeat one another, before venturing on any further attempt at a definition. In the various quotations thus far set down, Transcendentalism has been described from several apparently unrelated points of view. It is to be noted, however, that it is not so much the *sum* of all these various things as it is their *product*. It is one thing, and not many things. What gives New England Transcendentalism such importance as it has in the history of philosophy is simply that its philosophy is a consistent part of a larger whole.

Turning now to what this philosophy actually was, we find again a considerable variety of opinion. Some will have it that there was no philosophic content at all to New England Transcendentalism; while some express the fundamental principles with the greatest vagueness and indefiniteness, and others with absolute precision. What were the essential ideas upon which all the New England Transcendentalists were agreed? Was the diversity of opinion of the various members of the so-called "Transcendental Club" so great as to prevent their forming, in a modest way, a school of philosophy? And is there anything distinctive in New England Transcendentalism to separate it from the greater systems upon which it was founded?

The "fundamentals of Transcendentalism," says Cabot, "are to be

---

[15] Brownson, one of the most remarkable men of the group, felt the inevitable logic of this sequence; and thus, after he became a Romanist, he devoted a special essay to the thesis that "Protestantism ends in Transcendentalism." *Essays*, p. 209.

felt as sentiments, or grasped by the imagination as poetic wholes, rather than set down in propositions";[16] and Frances Tiffany, in one of the best definitions thus far formulated, says, "First and foremost, it can only be rightly conceived as an intellectual, aesthetic, and spiritual *ferment,* not a *strictly reasoned doctrine.* It was a Renaissance of conscious, living faith in the power of reason, in the reality of spiritual insight, in the privilege, beauty, and glory of life." [17] The utmost vagueness as to the philosophic content of Transcendentalism is to be found in the always quoted passages from Emerson's lecture on "The Transcendentalist," [18] and here and there in his Journals;[19] while Theodore Parker, on the other hand, who was to Emerson, in a way, what Ben Jonson was to Shakespeare, defines with scholarly exactitude while he misses the poetic largeness, the Gothic suggestiveness and freedom.[20] No account of the Transcendental philosophy could be more satisfactory and less adequate than Parker's. It leaves nothing distinctive, nothing original. The very harmlessness and sanity of his statement is what makes it false.

Where the two leading exponents of the school take such divergent views, it seems at first more than hazardous to attempt to say what position they all held in common, or even to assert that they were united by more than a personal friendship and "a common impatience of routine thinking." [21] But the writings of the various members of the group re-

---

[16] *A Memoir of Ralph Waldo Emerson,* I, 248.

[17] "Transcendentalism: The New England Renaissance," *Unitar. R.,* XXXI, III.

[18] "Transcendentalism is . . . Idealism as it appears in 1842. . . . The Transcendentalist adopts the whole connection of spiritual doctrine. . . . If there is anything grand or daring in human thought or virtue, any reliance on the vast, the unknown; any presentiment, any extravagance of faith, the spiritualist adopts it as most in nature. The oriental mind has always tended to this largeness. Buddhism is an expression of it. The Buddhist . . . is a Transcendentalist. . . . Shall we say then that Transcendentalism is the Saturnalia or excess of Faith; the presentiment of a faith proper to man in his integrity, excessive only when his imperfect obedience hinders the satisfaction of his wish?" *Works,* I, 317-320.

[19] In the lecture quoted above, Emerson refers to Kant's "transcendental forms" as a basis for New England Transcendentalism; but in his Journal he is more independent. Let one not consult the Germans, he says, but omit in his own mind what is added from tradition, "and the rest will be Transcendentalism." (Vol. VI, p. 380.)

[20] "That there is in the intellect (or consciousness), something that never was in the senses, to wit, the intellect (or consciousness) itself; that man has faculties which transcend the senses; faculties which give him ideas and intuitions that transcend sensational experiences; ideas whose origin is not from sense, nor their proof from sense." *Op. cit.,* p. 23.

[21] Cabot, I, 249. "We called ourselves the club of the like-minded, I suppose because no two of us thought alike," said James Freeman Clarke.

veal distinctly more than this. Let me attempt a brief statement of what they held in common.

As a group, or "school," the New England Transcendentalists thought, at least at the start, that they were followers of Kant in accepting a distinction between the reason and the understanding, and in attributing to the former the power of knowing truth directly.[22] Later, as they acquired some familiarity with other idealistic philosophies, they diverged somewhat in their thinking; but they all remained consistent in their belief that the world of spirit (or of some super-spiritual substance) was the groundwork of being and the material universe an appearance or effect; and that as the soul partook of the nature of God it had, through its highest quality as "reason," direct perception of reality. Beyond this, some members of the group did not care to venture.

So much of theory held in common would not entitle the New England Transcendentalists to any separate consideration in the history of philosophy. But these men were not content to let their newly acquired idealism remain sterile. As they had come to accept it because of its imaginative and emotional appeal, so they applied it with enthusiasm and vigor to the problems of actual life; and in doing this they felt that they were making a distinct forward step. Their attitude is well expressed in an anonymous contemporary dialogue. Mr. A, in endeavoring to explain his beliefs to Mr. B, remarks, "The Transcendentalists of our country . . . have made great advances upon the Kantean philosophy; we have . . . made it bear more directly upon the duties and relations of life." [23] It was their emphasis upon this practical application of their philosophy that has led so many of their critics to lose sight of their philosophy altogether.[24]

But it was not that the New England Transcendentalists applied their idealism in religion and conduct; it is rather that they took as a

---

[22] As early as 1839 this mistake was pointed out by one of the most vigorous critics of the time, the Rev. James Waddel Alexander, who remarked that Kant "simply meant to attribute to pure reason the power of directing the cognitive energy beyond its nearer objects, and to extend its research indefinitely; but by no means to challenge for this power the direct intuition of the absolute, as the veritable object of infallible insight," as is done "by some of our American imitators." *Princ. R.*, XI, 49.

[23] *New Englander*, I, 503.

[24] "It was a temper rather than a theory, an aspiration rather than a philosophy." W. M. Payne, *Leading American Essayists*, p. 187. This is the general, somewhat patronizing attitude which the average writer on the subject is wont to take.

test of idealism its practicability, that makes their distinctive contribution to philosophy. They asked of Transcendentalism not so much the age-old query, "Does it explain?" as the great modern question, *"Does it work?"* Philosophy that did not prove itself by this test had no warrant with them. The Transcendentalism of these men was a Pragmatic Mysticism. This of course did not imply that their system should be built up from such merely apparent things as *facts.* The data of experience had already been discredited as the stuff out of which the sensationalism of Locke was constructed.[25] No; that idealism was ennobling was its sufficient proof; that sensationalism was degrading in its influence was a complete refutation of John Locke.

For this emphasis on the practical and the moral, New England Transcendentalism was of course indebted to a Puritan inheritance.[26] In this, as in many other things, it was emphatically an American product, and could not have found its complete expression in any other land. Hecker, who was closely associated with the group at Brook Farm before he became a Romanist, contends very ably that Transcendentalism was merely an outgrowth of American Democracy;[27] and though he seems to forget that our democratic government and institutions were the result of religious freedom and not its cause, yet it is unquestionably true that without the aid of our political freedom this extreme expression of religious liberty could never have taken place. This local and particular character of Transcendentalism was realized at the time. Dickens, in his *American Notes,* says, "If I were a Bostonian, I think I would be a Transcendentalist." Ordinarily one's philosophy does not depend upon his *habitat.*

These, then, are the elements of which New England Transcendentalism was composed; and no definition would be complete that did not take account of all of them. Such a definition would be cumbersome and ungainly. Let us say, then, simply, that New England Transcendentalism was produced by the deliberate importing of certain imperfectly understood elements of German idealism into American Unitarianism; that it became a creative force in American life and letters; but that as a philosophy it was merely a sort of mystical idealism built on pragmatic

---

[25] When Hedge was told that the facts were against him, he replied, "So much the worse for the facts." Bartol: *Radical Problems,* p. 70.

[26] Transcendentalism, as embodied in its leaders, Alcott, Emerson, Parker, and Margaret Fuller, was—whatever else as well—"a blending of Platonic metaphysics and the Puritan spirit, of a philosophy and a character . . . taking place at a definite time, in a specially fertilized soil, under particular conditions." H. C. Goddard: *Studies in New England Transcendentalism,* pp. 189 and 196.

[27] *Catholic World,* XXIII, 534.

premises. This skeleton of a definition, if read in connection with the twenty representative comments I have quoted, will at least serve as a basis on which we may consider the philosophy of Emerson.

To attempt a statement of what Emerson's philosophy really was is a task as difficult as it is thankless. We have long been accustomed not only to rejecting him wholly as a philosopher, but also to placing upon him certain other values with which the establishment of a philosophical claim would interfere. The estimate which I have been forced to take of Emerson's contribution to philosophy far exceeds that which is usually put upon it; and though this may easily be due to the importance which a subject is wont to take upon near examination, yet I find that opinion in the scholarly world has grown rapidly of late years in this same direction. It is time that the main tenets of New England Transcendentalism received a definite philosophical statement; and these, without question, may best be noted in the central figure of the group. For whatever the value of Emerson's thought may have been, it is almost beyond dispute that there is no independent value in the philosophical aspirations of his associates.

Emerson bears much the same relation to the Transcendentalists of New England as Socrates bore to the Sophists of Athens: he was distinctly one of them, yet distinctly apart from the rest. Like Socrates, he had no system of philosophy to support; and like him, again, the results of his teaching were not theories but men. Or, to bring the comparison nearer, Emerson stands in much the same relation to the philosophy and religion of the nineteenth century as Jonathan Edwards, born just one hundred years before him, stands to the philosophy and religion of the eighteenth. These two men represent the extreme expression of their respective times. Each was a pure idealist, though neither was original in his system-making; both were men of high character and of great moral earnestness. Their vast difference of attitude is the concrete expression of the difference between Puritanism and Unitarianism.

The period of Transcendentalism in New England may be said to begin with the publication of Emerson's *Nature* in 1836. It is true that the "stir" was felt much earlier. Unitarianism entered into a new period of life and activity about 1815, with Channing and Walker as its leaders; and so clearly did these men foreshadow the later developments that they have sometimes, but without sufficient warrant, been counted as Transcendentalists. The first importation of the essential German contribution came with the return from Göttingen of Bancroft, Everett, and Ticknor; and one critic accordingly begins the period of Transcendentalism "about 1820." [28]   But the first genuine interest in German philosophy did not come with these men, but through English and French sources—through Coleridge and Cousin—and was not felt in New England till after 1830.   The direct and purposeful engrafting of German idealism upon American Unitarianism, by which New England Transcendentalism was really created, that is, the formation of the "Transcendental Club," took place in the very year that Emerson's *Nature* gave to it its first real utterance.   And it was in this same year that the American edition of Carlyle's *Sartor Resartus* brought to a head the growing spirit of unrest.[29] . With Emerson's *Nature* Transcendentalism found its first adequate expression not only in philosophy but in literature;[30] and it is accordingly from 1836 that Higginson and others have dated the beginning of a genuine and distinctive American literature.

It is less easy to fix upon a date, like "the closing of the theatres in 1642," which will conveniently mark the end of the period.   We might well choose the publication of Emerson's Second Series of *Essays* and of the last number of *The Dial* in 1844,[31] though Judd's *Margaret,* the one distinctive piece of Transcendental fiction, was not published till the following year, and the experiment at Brook Farm lasted two years longer. Or we might, with more liberality, bring down the period of Transcendentalism to the death of Thoreau in 1862, by which time Parker and Margaret Fuller had also died, and Emerson's *Conduct of Life* had virtually completed his contribution.   Even this would not include the work of such younger but thorough-going Transcendentalists as Higginson and Sanborn; while the publication of the first book of the originator of the "Transcendental Club" did not occur till 1865.[32]   Goblet d'Alviella, em-

---

[28] F. C. Lockwood: *Emerson as a Philosopher*, p. 3.

[29] "This was the signal for a sudden mental and moral mutiny," says Lowell, in his essay on Thoreau; and John Orr dates the Transcendental movement not from Emerson's book but from Carlyle's in the same year.

[30] The first important books of Alcott and of Ripley appeared also in 1836, and no other member of the group had published anything of consequence before this.

[31] *The Dial* contained representative work from all the leading members of the group: Emerson, Margaret Fuller, Ellery Channing (the poet), Thoreau, Parker, and Cranch were fully and adequately represented; while less frequent contributions were received from Alcott, James Freeman Clarke, W. H. Channing, Dwight, Ripley, Hedge, and Jones Very. Many of the less famous members are also included.   Between 1836 and 1844 books were published by Emerson, Alcott, Parker, Margaret Fuller, Ripley, Clarke, Cranch, Ellery Channing, and Jones Very. Thoreau's first book was not published till 1849.

[32] Hedge's *Reason in Religion.*

phasizing the practical and reformatory aspect of Transcendentalism, extends the period to include the Civil War.[33] It seems to me, however, that the publication of Emerson's *Poems,* and the breaking up of the Brook Farm experiment, in 1847, should be taken as more appropriately marking the close of the period than any of these later events, coming, as they did, when Transcendentalism had already become a declining rather than a growing force. Nothing essentially characteristic was added after Emerson's philosophy appeared again in the form of poetry; and the failure of Brook Farm marks the close of the second of the two notable undertakings which originated in the "Transcendental Club." *The Dial,* as I have said, was already suspended. I venture, therefore, to name the years 1836 to 1847 as those we should accept in marking out the period of New England Transcendentalism.

The development of American Unitarianism to the point where it could furnish a proper soil for Transcendentalism is best told in connection with the life and influence of William Ellery Channing; the introduction or rather domesticating of German philosophy, which brought New England Transcendentalism itself into being, was the work, mainly, of Frederick Henry Hedge.

---

[33] *Contemporary Evolution of Religious Thought,* pp. 176 f.

CHAPTER I.

BEGINNINGS OF NEW ENGLAND TRANSCENDENTALISM: CHANNING AND
THE UNITARIAN MOVEMENT; HEDGE AND THE
"TRANSCENDENTAL CLUB."

William Ellery Channing was born in the year 1780. It is not a
little remarkable that the decade of his birth should have been that
which not only witnessed the birth of Unitarianism in this country, but
which marked the beginning of those three great movements in Germany,
England, and France which were the determining factors of the Transcendental movement of New England. I mean, of course, the remarkable development of German idealism dating from the publication of
Kant's *Critique* in 1781; the rise of English Romanticism heralded by
the appearance of the songs of Burns in 1786; and the political and
social revolutions which began in France with the fall of the Bastille in
1789. It was Channing's mission, more than that of any other man, to
prepare the New England of Jonathan Edwards to become the New
England of Emerson.

Channing is the connecting link between these two men and their
strangely dissimilar periods. It was only because he was firmly grounded
in the old theology that he was able to lead almost the entire thinking
population of Boston to a readiness to accept the new. He was ordained
in Boston in 1803, the year of the birth of Emerson and of the death of
Samuel Hopkins, who was the greatest of Edwards' disciples and the
man who was both Channing's teacher and the immediate cause of his
revolt from the Edwardian theology. From this date until the decided
appearance of Emerson and Parker, Channing was the dominant influence in American religious history.

The story of his enlightenment is well known. While reading
Hutcheson he came upon the sudden realization that if man is truly the
child of God he must be free as God is free.[34] Old as the thought was,
it marked an epoch in our religious history. From this "discovery"

---

[34] If he deduced this from reading Hutcheson it must have been by his con-
troversial instinct, for Hutcheson was a determinist. But this author's teaching of
man's capacity for disinterested affection was quite in line with the thought of
Hopkins, and consequently with Channing's habit of mind. This was probably the
starting-point of his later thinking.

until he spoke his dying words, "I have received many messages from the Spirit," Channing stood for the freedom of the individual to think for himself in matters of religion.

But so long as the assertion of the right of individual judgment meant no more than the ability of the soul to receive "these supernatural solicitings," it differed little from the faith of many religious persons of the past; for the experience which they interpreted as illumination has come to almost all sensitively constructed religious persons. The doctrine of the "inner light" as taught by George Fox and the Quakers of this country, was an especially obnoxious heresy to the Puritans because it differed so little from their own belief. But Channing's love of freedom was closely bound up with the revolutions of France, and from this it received a certain breadth and motive power which enabled him to take a much firmer hold upon the children of the men who had engaged in the Boston Tea Party.[35] As late as 1830 he was carried away with enthusiasm over the three days' revolution of July, and proportionately indignant at the general indifference in Boston. "I was a young man in college in the days of the first French Republic," he said, "and at every crisis in its history our dignity was wholly upset. We were rushing to meetings of sympathy or kindling bonfires of congratulation and walking in torchlight processions." On being called a young man for still showing this spirit, "he answered in a loud, ringing tone that was almost an hurrah, 'Always young for liberty!' "[36]

But the influence of Channing was the most important factor in bringing about the change of attitude which resulted in Transcendentalism, not only because of his insistence upon the right of private judgment in matters of religion, nor even because he enforced this in the spirit of a staunch advocate of freedom; but because his strong literary sense and commanding eloquence supplied the motive power that was needed. No appeal was possible to the Boston to which Channing came but that which was made in the form of art. Channing appealed to that literary sense of largeness, of elevation, of profound suggestion which

---

[35] "This emphasis on the soul and its rights," says Mr. Daniel Dulany Addison, speaking of Channing's belief in the worth of the individual man, "was in direct contrast to previous New England theological thinking and caused the repudiation of the teaching of Edwards and Hopkins. Channing was more under the influence of the writers of the French Revolution than the Puritan Fathers." (*The Clergy in American Life and Letters*, p. 200.)

[36] William W. Fenn, in *Pioneers of Religious Liberty in America*, p. 187. Given also, with slight variations, in the *Life of William Ellery Channing* by his nephew, W. H. Channing, p. 601, Hedge's *Martin Luther and Other Essays*, p. 170, and elsewhere.

England had been developing during her whole romantic movement. "Channing rose out of the reign of opinions into that of ideas," says James Freeman Clarke.[37] Without being able to think profoundly for himself, he was fascinated, and in turn fascinated his hearers, with a certain breadth and elevation of thought. His purely literary articles, published between 1825 and 1830, are of importance because of the great impression which they produced.[38] But in his familiarity with Wordsworth and Coleridge, and in his love for them and more critical estimate of their associates, Channing had at least an appreciation of English Romanticism which was keen, and an expression of it in his own work which was adequate.

If our estimate of the causes which produced Transcendentalism has been corect, and if Channing brought to American Unitarianism an appreciation of the French and English elements to the extent we have seen, then nothing remained but an acceptance of German Idealism to make him the first of the Transcendentalists. That he had some knowledge of German philosophy, even a large amount of sympathy with it, must be granted. "It was with intense delight," says his nephew, "that he made acquaintance with the master minds of Germany, through the medium, first of Madame de Staël, and afterwards of Coleridge." After speaking of his enthusiasm for Kant, Schelling, and Fichte, the biographer adds: "Without adopting the systems of either of these philosophers, and, fortunately perhaps for him, without being fully acquainted with these systems, he yet received from their examples the most animating incentives to follow out the paths of speculation into which his own mind had entered." [39]

Yet Channing was far from being a philosopher, and it was because of this lack that his religious inconsistencies gave way before the keen logic of Theodore Parker, and led to the ultimate triumph of Transcendentalism over the earlier Unitarianism.[40] Channing had spoken

---

[37] *Memorial and Biographical Sketches,* p. 158.

[38] Mr. John White Chadwick apologizes for the taste of Channing's contemporaries by calling attention to the state of American literature at this time. "But when Channing's articles appeared there was no such 'mob of gentlemen who write with ease' and write extremely well as we have now. Judged by purely literary standards, hundreds of these write better than Channing. But 'in the country of the blind, the one-eyed man is king,' and it is not strange that under the general conditions that prevailed from 1825 to 1830 Channing's literary product earned for him the enthusiastic admiration of his co-religionists and of many who were not joined to their assembly." (*William Ellery Channing: Minister of Religion,* p. 196.)

[39] *Life of William Ellery Channing,* by his nephew, W. H. Channing, p. 175.

[40] "He admitted the resurrection of Jesus," says Renan, "but not his divinity;

for the right of private judgment in religion, with the deep conviction of a great advocate of freedom, and with the lofty tone of a poet; and in making the receptivity of the soul a universal attribute, though he had not himself enlarged it to a philosophy, he had at least created the need of a philosophical warrant for this old doctrine.

This need was deeply felt and to some extent supplied by James Walker (1794-1874). The claims of this vigorous old theologian to some consideration in any treatment of the beginnings of Transcendentalism in New England are so great that we may well consider whether in bringing a greater philosophical interest and knowledge to bear on the Unitarian position he was not indeed the first of the Transcendentalists.

Walker was next to Channing the most important champion of the "Liberal" movement of 1815. Like Channing he was impulsive and enthusiastic in his youth, though there is little in the published sermons of either one to suggest that this could ever have been the case. As Professor of Moral Philosophy at Harvard, of which he was afterwards President, and as editor of the *Christian Examiner,* he had much to do with moulding the spirit of the age.

Although Walker was a devout Christian, believing in the established means of grace and approving of philosophy only as serving the ends of religion, yet he had a strong grasp on the problems of philosophy and a deep interest in them; so that he is often spoken of by his younger contemporaries as a metaphysician. But as Frothingham well points out, his mind seems to have been of an emphatically English cast, rather than German or French. And so, though he studied conscientiously the German philosophers from Kant to Hegel, as well as Cousin and Jouffroy, he did not fully enter into their spirit, nor find in them the spiritual element he wanted. His apparent reason, from his own English point of view, is expressed pithily in his remark, "Good sense *must* be; other things *may* be, good sense *must* be;"—a remark which must be read in the light of his later comment, "Men may put down Transcendentalism if they can, but they must first deign to comprehend its principles."

Frothingham speaks of Walker as taking the Transcendental position out and out in 1834,[41] two years before the date we have assigned to its first expression, and as evidence quotes from his once famous ser-

___

he admitted the Bible but not hell." Channing tried to hold to both the divinity and humanity of Jesus; but why not, as Renan says, "frankly call him divine? It requires no more effort to believe one than the other." (*Études d'Histoire Religieuse,* p. 378.) It was this central inconsistency that Parker perceived and condemned.

41 *Transcendentalism in New England,* p. 120.

mon on "The Philosophy of Man's Spiritual Nature in regard to the Foundations of Faith." [42]   But in this sermon Walker was only endeavoring to establish "the existence and reality *of the spiritual world"* (his whole sentence is in italics), from "the acknowledged existence and reality of spiritual impressions or perceptions"; and in order to state his point "in the simplest and clearest language of which the subject is susceptible," he explains,—"just as, from the acknowledged existence and reality of sensible impressions or perceptions, we may and do assume the existence and realities of the sensible world." [43]   This is quite the opposite of Transcendentalism. It is true that in this same sermon he expresses the hope for "a better philosophy than the degrading sensualism, out of which most forms of modern infidelity have grown . . . a philosophy which recognizes the higher nature of man . . . which comprehends the soul . . . which continually reminds us of our intimate relationship to the spiritual world." [44]   But though this was most valuable in determining the tendencies of the time, it is not the realization or presentation of Transcendentalism ·itself.   Frothingham comes nearer to a just statement of Walker's position when he says, writing at a later time, that he transferred "the sanctions of authority from outward to inward, from external testimony to immediate consciousness, from the senses to the soul, as the deepest thinkers in all ages have done. . . . He attributed to the soul a receptive but not a creative power."[45]

German philosophy had been introduced into France by the *Allemagne* of Madame de Staël, and though this book had been somewhat noticed and read both in this country and England, it received small notice in France till Cousin began to incorporate parts of it in his philosophy.   Cousin's influence in America began when his *Introduction to History of Philosophy* was translated by H. G. Linberg and published in Boston in 1832, and more especially when, two years later, his *History of Philosophy in the Eighteenth Century,* containing his vigorous criticism of Locke, was translated and published with an elaborate introduction by Caleb Sprague Henry, under the title *Elements of Psychology.*[46]

---

[42] This sermon, printed in the *Christian Examiner* and republished as a tract, may be found in Walker's volume of sermons entitled *Reason, Faith and Duty.*

[43] *Reason, Faith and Duty,* p. 39.

[44] *Ibid.,* pp. 60, 61.

[45] *Atlantic Monthly,* LII, 18.

[46] "Linberg's translation of Cousin's *Introduction to History of Philosophy* may be considered as the great store-house, from which most of them—e. g., Brownson, Emerson, Parker, &c.—have derived their peculiar philosophical opinions, their modes of reasoning, and their forms of thought and expression." *American Church R.,* XIX, 411.

But notable as was the influence of Cousin, that of Coleridge was certainly greater. In 1829 the *Aids to Reflection* was published with an introduction by James Marsh, who proposed Kant, Jacobi, the English Platonists, and Coleridge as a substitute for the current philosophy. In 1833 Frederick Henry Hedge wrote a review of this book,[47] and at once brought the contribution of Coleridge to a focus. This review was called by him later "the first word, as far as I know, which any American had uttered in respectful recognition of the claims of Transcendentalism."[48] It is Hedge's Unitarian point of view that gives this review its significance for our study. Of Coleridge he writes: "He appears as a zealous Trinitarian and a warm defender of the doctrines of the English church. We have no doubt of his sincerity; but unless we err greatly he has either misunderstood his own views, or grossly misrepresented the doctrines of his church."[49]

But the personal influence of Hedge himself had, I believe, more to do with popularizing German philosophy in the transcendental group than had either the vague Coleridge or the glittering Cousin. Hedge had received his training in the German schools, and to a considerable extent he knew the mighty Germans in their own language. As minister at West Cambridge from 1829 till 1835, he came in contact with all the members of the group; and during these formative years he seems to have made them familiar with the main conceptions of Kant, Fichte, and Schelling. Of Hegel, neither Hedge nor his friends knew very much, at this time or later. The influence of the German ideas, which Hedge was able to state with comparative correctness, in the daily conversation of intelligent and thoughtful men and women, is hard to estimate, and has been largely neglected because, of course, it was left unrecorded. In 1834 Emerson wrote in his Journal, "Hedge read me good things out of Schleiermacher;"[50] and a little later, "Coleridge loses . . . by his own concealing, uncandid acknowledgement of debt to Schelling,"[51] which indicates that he now knew more of Schelling than Coleridge had to teach him. Yet Cabot, who knew whereof he spoke, says, with reference

---

[47] Together with *The Friend,* republished at Burlington, Vermont, in 1831. *Christian Examiner,* XIV, 108.

[48] Quoted by Mrs. Dall in her *Transcendentalism in New England,* p. 15. In this review Hedge praises the work of Marsh; then, after commenting on Kant and Fichte, he considers Schelling as "the most satisfactory." Coleridge he regards as a profound thinker, though not a successful poet.

[49] *Christian Examiner,* XIV, 127. To Emerson, Coleridge's churchmanship was merely "a harmless freak." *Journals,* IV, 152.

[50] *Journals,* III, 393.

[51] *Journals,* III, 503.

especially to Fichte and Schelling, "I had reason to believe that he had no first-hand acquaintance with the books."

Hedge's own knowledge of German philosophy was by no means systematic or profound, and his influence would not have been so great if it had been. "This atmosphere, rather than any form and understanding merely, of German thought," says the editor of the *Unitarian Review*, "rather than any formal teaching of philosophy,—which he disbelieved in and kept aloof from,—made his characteristic service to our so-called 'Transcendental' movement." [52]   For Cabot's invaluable *Memoir* of Emerson, Hedge wrote an account of the origin of the "Transcendental Club," which shows how the influence of German philosophy was first brought to bear upon American Unitarianism:

"In September, 1836, on the day of the second centennial anniversary of Harvard College, Mr. Emerson, George Ripley, and myself, with one other,[53] chanced to confer together on the state of current opinion in theology and philosophy, which we agreed in thinking very unsatisfactory. . . . What we strongly felt was dissatisfaction with the reigning sensuous philosophy, dating from Locke, on which our Unitarian theology was based. The writings of Coleridge, recently edited by Marsh, and some of Carlyle's earlier essays, especially the 'Characteristics' and 'Signs of the Times,' had created a ferment in the minds of some of the young clergy of that day. We four concluded to call a few like-minded seekers together on the following week. Some dozen of us met in Boston, in the house, I believe, of Mr. Ripley. . . . These were the earliest of a series of meetings held from time to time, as occasion prompted, for seven or eight years."

---

[52] "A Memory of Dr. Hedge" [By J. H. Allen], *Unitar. R.*, XXXIV, 269.

[53] This was George Putnam. But he was not fully in sympathy with the movement, and did not attend after the first meeting.

CHAPTER II.

EMERSON: HIS PHILOSOPHICAL ATTITUDE AND METHOD.

The life of Emerson has been so often told that it needs no restating. One hesitates to say again that "the blood of eight generations of ministers flowed in his veins." But this is a most important thing to notice in any study of his philosophy. Emerson approached philosophy with a religious attitude. If one hesitates also to say again that after being ordained as a Unitarian minister in Boston in 1829, Emerson resigned his charge four years later because of his unwillingness to administer the ordinance of the Lord's Supper, and continued thenceforth, with the beauty and serenity of a great character, to announce from the lecture platform his inspiring spiritual perceptions, still it must not be forgotten that this was the other side of the same matter,—Emerson approached religion with the attitude of a philosopher. No philosophy was possible to him without its having a basis in religious instinct; no religious faith or form could be accepted that had not its justification in the light of reason. In his mind the two were neither separate nor separable.

If his attitude toward religion is the first thing to note in gaining a correct point of view for estimating Emerson's philosophy, his attitude toward practical conduct has also its importance in enabling us to read him with that sympathy which is essential to any sort of justice. Not philosophy for its own sake, but philosophy for its bearing on the life of men was ever in his eye, and it is on this account that he can be read without previous philosophical training. His "practical idealism" was reflected most remarkably in his life. We could not think of Emerson as living in stateliness and ease, for his teachings of heroism, of prudence, of the homely virtues, would make this ridiculous; nor yet as surrounded by scenes of embittering and debasing poverty, for his wholesome, ever-smiling optimism would then have been impossible, even to him. It is evident enough, also, that he could not have entered into the Brook Farm or Fruitlands experiments, for his shrewd Yankee sense glints forth at every turn; nor yet could he have turned away coldly from such noble dreams of world regeneration, for his humor was ever more kindly than keen, his hopes always above his expectations. And so, again, Emerson could never join in the excited tumult of the Abolitionists, for his soul was calm and his faith mighty; yet the murder of Lovejoy and the desertion of Webster roused him to indignation. In all this we note a certain aloofness caused by his serenity, or his optimism, or that chilliness of temperament of which Margaret Fuller complained and to which he dolefully but blandly confessed; and side by side with this we find a philosophy of which one of the main essentials was the dependence of pure thought upon practical conduct.

It is not, however, its religious or its pragmatic aspects that have caused Emerson's philosophy to be charged with a fundamental ama-teurishness—if I may so say—a lack of system, of philosophical con-sistency, indeed of that logical soundness which is essential to an orig-inal thinker worthy of any serious consideration. There is no need to remind the philosophic world that Emerson was primarily a poet. Even, indeed especially, in his prose, it is ever the poet who is speaking. We have here just the reverse of those ancient philosophers who reasoned out their systems in the form of verse; we have the appearance of philosophy but the soul of poetry. The characteristic of the poet is en-thusiasm, which leads him, in his great delight over the discovery of any new truth to state it with the exaggeration which his high emotion leads him to assume. "Language overstates," says Emerson (I, 190); and the freedom of his own prose form leads him to extreme overstatement. "I would put myself in the attitude to look in the eye of abstract truth, and I cannot. I blench and withdraw on this side and on that" (II, 309). The question must inevitably occur, Does Emerson remain a man of let-ters, merely, who dabbled in philosophy, or is he a philosopher who chose, as the mighty Plato himself had chosen, to reformulate the thoughts of his predecessors and give them an artistic rendering?

No one who wished well by Emerson would press an analogy to Plato, whose greatness as a philosopher so easily transcended whatever limitations he may have had. But that Emerson had a right conception of philosophy, and worked at it not as a literary dilettante but with the seriousness of one deeply concerned with the problems themselves, must be recognized fully if we are to secure for our subject a fair hearing. So widespread is the belief that Emerson's inconsistencies are funda-mental, his want of logic and system a congenital defect, and hence his contribution to philosophy merely an imaginative restatement with some sort of mystical interpretation of various suggestive thinkers whom he had read at haphazard, that I may be pardoned for adding to my own conviction to the contrary the authority of some whose names cannot fail to give pause to those who have too hastily assumed the truth of these singular impeachments.

Not wholly singular, one must admit, since Emerson himself in certain famous phrases has encouraged the belief. The "infinitely repellent particles" to which in playful modesty he compared his sentences in an often quoted letter to Carlyle, at once caught the popular imagination and comforted some who have found themselves on a first reading puzzled and annoyed. "A foolish consistency is the hobgoblin of little minds" (II, 58) is usually quoted without the word "foolish," and I have now and again heard this splendid manifesto of the truth-seeker turned against the philosopher. But it may be said that Emerson expressly denied his ability to use "that systematic form which is reckoned essential in treating the science of the mind" (XII, 11), and that indeed he goes so far as to say, "The moment it [Logic] would appear as propositions and have a separate value, it is worthless" (II, 507); and how can one claim standing as a system-maker who says naïvely, "I know better than to claim any completeness for the picture. I am a fragment, and this is a fragment of me" (III, 83),—"I simply experiment, an endless seeker with no Past at my back" (II, 297)? But all this, so far as it was not mere modesty, came from a wise caution, and an almost morbid horror of stifling truth by forcing it into set and definite terms.[54] It was on this account that he could say so blandly to a doubting follower, "Very well; I do not wish disciples";[55] for I believe that Emerson would have felt the founding of a school an impeachment on his honesty —a closing of the windows that looked toward heaven. With all deference to the mighty Kant, no phrase would have given him a keener pain than "Aber Emerson sagt." It should be evident to anyone who feels competent to criticize Emerson's want of consistency and system that his own confession of it comes to no more than a perpetual openness of mind to receive new truth, coupled with a skeptical attitude toward the acquiring of definite results by too formal a method. But Emerson was no cheap radical, no mere iconoclast in his unsystematic method. "I would gladly be moral," he comments by the way, "and keep due metes and bounds, which I dearly love, and allow the most to the will of man; but I have set my heart on honesty in this chapter" (III, 71). And on honesty his heart was set no less in every chapter he wrote.

But it soon became a tradition to consider Emerson from the point of view to which his confessions, or rather boasts, of inconsistency and

---

[54] In this he anticipated Ibsen, who felt that a particularly vital truth might live for perhaps twenty years before becoming false! See *An Enemy of the People.*

[55] Charles J. Woodbury's *Talks with Ralph Waldo Emerson,* p. 60.

formlessness so easily laid him open. Lowell, whose picturesqueness of phrase often makes his merest witticism memorable, wrote in his essay on "Emerson the Lecturer" [56] of "a chaos full of shooting stars, a jumble of creative forces"; and the poets and men of letters who have followed Lowell in judging Emerson have usually been impressed, as Lowell was, by the greatness of his mind and the imperfection of his sense of form, which latter they have rather assumed than proven kept Emerson from taking any place in the ranks of the real philosophers. Thus Holmes, in that delightful book on Emerson which has been called "the biography of a wood thrush by a canary bird," when the moment comes in which he should state the value of Emerson's thought contents himself with saying, "He was a man of intuition, of insight, a seer, a poet, with a tendency to mysticism." [57]   And Woodberry, who disclaiming intellectual sympathy with Emerson can still say, "I feel in his work the presence of a great mind. His is the only great mind that America has produced in literature," [58] still has it as his final verdict that Emerson is to be regarded only as a poet. More outspoken, indeed overtly denunciatory, is Richard Garnett: "He could see, but he could not prove; he could announce, but he could not argue. His intuitions were his sole guide; what they revealed appeared to him self-evident; the ordinary paths by which men arrive at conclusions were closed to him. To those in spiritual sympathy with himself he is not only fascinating, but authoritative; his words authenticate themselves by the response they awake in the breast. But the reader who will have reasons gets none, save reason to believe that the oracle is an imposition." [59]   Thus we see that the tradition of Emerson's inability to reason in the manner of even an ordinary thinker is well established among his literary followers; the same sort of criticism may still be found in such writers as Mr. Paul Elmore More (*Shelbourne Essays*) and Mr. Van Wyck Brooks (*America's Coming of Age*).

True, statements to this effect by more philosophic writers are not wanting, from the tirade evoked by the First Series of Essays in the *Biblical Repository and Princeton Review* [60] to the dissertation of Mr.

---

[56] *Works*, I, 353.

[57] American Men of Letters: *Emerson*, p. 390.

[58] English Men of Letters: *Emerson*, p. 176.

[59] Great Writers: *Emerson*, p. 93.

[60] Vol. XIII, p. 539. The anonymous reviewer says that Emerson's is "the obscurity not of a deep but of a muddy stream, and the brilliancy of the surface is little else than the iridescence on a bowl of soap-bubbles. . . . From beginning to end there is a total absence of coherence and unity."

Charles M. Bakewell;[61] and even Emerson's co-religionists have at times patronized or condoned.[62]

But while it would be "special pleading" and hence false pleading (on behalf of a man who would have scorned such friendly consolation with all the fervor of a Job) to deny the manifest inconsistencies of Emerson where occasionally they do occur, or bring in only the evidence of those who will testify that these inconsistencies are inconsequential and that Emerson's command of logic was not only real but of a high order, still I cannot but feel that these latter, both by the nature of their testimony and their right to judge, should have put this matter forever beyond dispute. I shall mention merely in passing some of the literary and religious writers who have borne witness to Emerson's intellectual faculties, and then pass to those whose main interest is in philosophy, since they have here, surely, most right to speak.

In a delightful account of how Emerson endeavored (and all in vain) to induce him to abandon his peculiar type of verse, Walt Whitman recounts.[63] "It was an argument-statement, reconnoitering, review, attack, and pressing home (like an army corps in order, artillery, cavalry, infantry) . . . no judge's charge ever more complete or convincing." Passing over Mr. John Burroughs' obvious though generally neglected comment that certain of the essays "have more logical sequence and evolution than certain others," [64] let me refer only to the latest, as it is the best, of the statements by Emerson's more literary champions. Mr. O. W. Firkins in his recent delightfully written book devotes considerable space to a thorough-going defense of Emerson's very logic. His conclusion is: "Emerson, then, is disinclined to logic; he does not care to be delayed or bored. But the folly of critics, encouraged by a word of his own, has converted this disinclination into incapacity." [65] Mr. Firkins cites various instances of Emerson's "consecutive and logical reasoning."

---

[61] "The Philosophy of Emerson," Phil. R., XII, 530. I find nothing, however, in this essay which tends toward the establishment of the point in hand.

[62] "He is not a logical writer," said the nothing-if-not-logical Theodore Parker, though as always the mere assertion is allowed to stand. "We must not expect a seer to be an organizer," says Bartol, "any more than . . . an astronomer an engineer. We must supplement his calling, extend his vision, and perhaps correct his view."

[63] Specimen Days, p. 172.

[64] Indoor Studies, p. 145.

[65] Firkins' Emerson, p. 299. This book is deserving of especial praise. Even the chapter on "Emerson's Philosophy" is excellent, though less satisfactory than the rest. It is curious that Mr. Firkins, who insists so strongly upon Emerson's consecutiveness and coherence, should be more inconsecutive and incoherent than Emerson himself in this crucial chapter.

If, for the sake of completeness, we were now to record the religious vote, we should find that there are abundant statements, both from friends and foes, to show that Emerson's analytical ability was fully recognized. It will be sufficient if I cite a single comment from each camp. Says Edwin D. Mead: "This rare consistency and persistency is the ever notable thing in Emerson. It is the superficial man that finds and talks of inconsistencies in Emerson." [66] And the Rev. S. Law Wilson writes: "In moments of simple insight and pure intuition a man does not employ the scholastic terms and philosophic distinctions that Emerson does. . . . Evidently the Seer brought down with him from his Watch-tower of Contemplation very little that he did not take up with him." [67]

Emerson's method is treated with most respect by his most scholarly critics. Professor Dewey says, in writing of Emerson as the "Philosopher of Democracy," [68] "I am not acquainted with any writer, no matter how assured his position in treatises upon the history of philosophy, whose movement of thought is more compact and unified, nor one who combines more adequately diversity of intellectual attack with concentration of form and effort." Professor Münsterberg says that his sentences—those infinitely repellent particles—"are not only in harmony with each other, they are in deepest harmony with the spirit of modern philosophy." [69] Tyndall thought that "Emerson was a splendid manifestation of reason in its most comprehensive form"; and Grimm, more nearly than anyone else, has explained both how the impression of Emerson's inconsecutiveness exists, and what is the attitude of those who defend him: "At first one can detect no plan, no order, and we seek wonderingly for the hidden connection of these sentences. . . . Soon, however, we discover the deep underlying law according to which these thoughts are evolved, and the strict sequence." [70] And what that law is, is beautifully illustrated by Horace Mann in a letter quoted by Mr. Conway: [71] "As a man stationed in the sun would see all the planets moving around in one direction and in perfect harmony, while to an eye on the earth their motions are full of crossings and retrogressions, so he, from his central position in the spiritual world, discovers order and harmony where others can discern only confusion and irregularity." Emerson himself was as conscious of the underlying consistency of his thinking as he was of its superficial discrepancies. Immediately after the pas-

---

[66] *Genius and Character of Emerson*, p. 236.

[67] *The Theology of Modern Literature*, p. 105.

[68] *International Journal of Ethics*, 1903, p. 405.

[69] Harvard Psych. Studies, vol. II, p. 17.

[70] *Essays on Literature*, p. 25.

[71] *Emerson at Home and Abroad*, p. 149.

sage I referred to above (p. 27), where he admits that he cannot use "that systematic form which is reckoned essential in treating the science of the mind," he continues: "But if one can say so without arrogance, I might suggest that he who contents himself with dotting a fragmentary curve, recording only what facts he has observed, without attempting to arrange them within one outline, follows a system also,—a system as grand as any other. . . . I confess to a little distrust of that completeness of system which metaphysicians are apt to affect" (XII, 11).

It has seemed to me essential to state the case at this tiresome length because without a substantial agreement in this matter it is impossible to consider Emerson's philosophy with that fundamental respect which is essential to any sort of justice; and I have been forced to present as fairly as I could the consensus of opinion on the subject because it is not a matter for analysis or for argument. I may now only trust that anyone who may look through the statement that I am about to make of Emerson's philosophy will do so with exactly the same attitude that he would if this were an introduction to the philosophy of Schelling.

For it is to Schelling, of course, that Emerson is closest akin. Mr. John S. Harrison [72] throws the whole emphasis upon his reading of Plato and the Neo-Platonists, and Mr. Firkins concurs. Professor Riley says that Emerson's "knowledge of German metaphysic was slight and secondary";[73] and Cabot himself said definitely this same thing. On the other hand Mr. Lockwood claims the direct influence of Schelling,[74] and Mr. Goddard more guardedly and with more warrant speaks of the striking similarity between Emerson's thought and Coleridge's, and consequently between Emerson's and Schelling's, and shows successfully, it seems to me, that this was a more vitally stimulating if less continuous influence than that of Plato and the Neo-Platonists.[75]

But while Emerson was no doubt stimulated either directly by Schelling or indirectly through Coleridge, there can be no doubt that he was an original thinker, and arrived at his conclusions by very much the same methods as all other philosophers have done, however much he may have attributed a religious connotation to any new truth which he felt that he had acquired.[76] His purpose was not to make a system

---

[72] *The Teachers of Emerson.* New York: Sturgis and Walton, 1910.

[73] *American Thought*, p. 159.

[74] *Emerson as a Philosopher*, pp. 6, 7.

[75] *Studies in New England Transcendentalism*, pp. 80, 81.

[76] "There can be no greater blunder," says Mr. John M. Robertson in his *Modern Humanists* (p. 120), "than to suppose that men who use the analytic method begin to get notions by analysing mechanically. The act of analysis is itself a reaching forward identical in character with what Emerson called the secret augury."

which would stand with or supplement the systems before him, but simply to answer for himself those "obstinate questionings" with which we are all concerned in our deepest moments. It may be too much to say that Emerson would have arrived at just the same results if Schelling had not written; but a man of Emerson's open-mindedness, so free with his quotations, so eager indeed to attribute his own ideas to other men, could never have announced his "discoveries" in the hesitating, awestruck manner in which he gives them forth, if he had not thought them revealed to him in those sacred moments when he felt himself to be "part and parcel of God" (I, 16). The question of his indebtedness, therefore, seems to me to be of little moment.

Here, then, is material for a system,—shall we say?—and if we can arrange it in some sort of order, that of itself may enable us to see more clearly what value it may have. So ordered and systematized it will doubtless prove unsatisfactory; but there may be some gain,—perhaps enough to compensate for the loss. But no one will claim for it finality, and Emerson least of all. In the following chapter I shall attempt a statement of Emerson's answer to the question, "What is Reality?" Then I shall proceed to his answer to the question, "How is this explanation of Reality possible?" In recognizing the inconsistencies in his answer to this second question and in putting together the suggestions of what seems to me his final theory, I trust that I am not going farther than there is warrant for in those passages which, though fragmentary and imperfect, still give us genuine suggestions of what he intended as his final word. In order to do this, it will often be necessary to translate him into the language of philosophy. But it is a thankless task to put Emerson's conceptions into the stiff terms of the metaphysicians, and I shall endeavor to keep him as much as possible in his own beautiful "original." There is danger, also, with so vague and suggestive a writer, of reading into him the ideas in one's own mind; therefore with no more comment than is needed, I shall allow him to speak for himself, and as often as what he says offers its own explanation. It shall be my attempt to think through the subject in what seems to me Emerson's own plan; but I shall attempt to arrange in some sort of logical order the various difficulties which presented themselves to his mind, and to state expressly the steps by which he seems to have arrived, sometimes unconsciously to himself, at his more significant "discoveries." In doing this I must crave some patience, especially at the outset of the following discussion, for the reiteration of much that is both obvious and as old as thought itself.

CHAPTER III.

The Philosophy of Emerson: Nature, the Over-Soul, and the
Individual.

"A noble doubt perpetually suggests itself," writes Emerson in
his first published work, "whether this end [Discipline] be not the Final
Cause of the Universe; and whether nature outwardly exists" (I, 52).
The cause of this doubt is "my utter impotence to test the authenticity
of the report of my senses, to know whether the impressions they make
on me correspond with outlying objects." In spite of its age and obvious-
ness, this, as the starting point of Emerson's philosophy, is a point of
view on which he always insists, and to which he never hesitates to
recur. "The senses interfere everywhere, and mix their own structure
with all they report of" (VI, 295). "Souls never touch their objects.
. . . Dream delivers us to dream, and there is no end to illusion. . . .
There are moods in which we court suffering, in the hope that here at
least we shall find reality" (III, 52, 53). But though this is generally a
matter of mood and impression, Emerson's conclusion is as sane as it is
inevitable: there is no way of knowing what nature is, so, "Be it what
it may, it is ideal to me so long as I cannot try the accuracy of my
senses" (I, 53).

But this does not affect the "stability of nature." The great reality
is there, always ready for us to come to it when we will, and to interpret
it and enjoy it as Nature (III, 53). Indeed it is our place to come more
and more into association with Nature. In calling it "illusion" we do
not affect its practical reality in the least. "We come to our own and
make friends with matter, which the ambitious clatter of the schools
would persuade us to despise. We can never part with it; the mind
loves its old home" (III, 165). "Whether nature enjoy a substantial existence without, or is only the apocalypse of the mind, it is alike useful
and alike venerable to me" (I, 53).

Then if nature is illusion and its laws are permanent, what is the
reality which imposes these laws? The answer is obvious. "It is the
uniform effect of culture on the human mind, not to shake our faith in
the stability of particular phenomena, as of heat, water, azote; but to
lead us to regard nature as phenomenon, not a substance; to attribute

necessary existence to spirit; to esteem nature as an accident and an effect" (I, 54). This is the second obvious point in Emerson's Idealism, and this also he is never weary of restating. "On this power, this all-dissolving unity, the emphasis of heaven and earth is laid. Nature is brute but as the soul quickens it; Nature always the effect, mind the flowing cause" (VIII, 212).

But this indiscriminate use of "spirit" and of "mind" as the cause of nature leads to the further question, Of what spirit or mind is nature the effect? The first answer seems to be that the source is purely human. "The Intellect builds the Universe and is the key to all it contains" (XII, 4). "Every law in nature, as gravity, centripetence, repulsion, polarity, undulation, has a counterpart in the intellect" (VIII, 211); and on this "perfect parallelism between the laws of Nature and the laws of thought" (VIII, 13) is based this third development of Emerson's thinking according to the order in which I am trying to arrange it. His statement of this position is very frequent,—sometimes rhetorical, sometimes absolute, and sometimes argumentative. "What if you shall come to realize that the play and the playground of all this pompous history are radiations from yourself, and that the sun borrows his beams?" (VI, 302). "Man is always throwing his praise or blame on events, and does not see that he only is real, and the world his mirror and echo" (X, 185). "We have learned that we do not see directly, but mediately, and that we have no means of correcting these colored and distorting lenses which we are, or of computing the amount of their errors. Perhaps these subject-lenses have a creative power; perhaps there are no objects. Once we lived in what we saw; now the rapaciousness of this new power, which threatens to absorb all things, engages us. Nature, art, persons, letters, religion, objects, successively tumble in, and God is but one of its ideas. Nature and literature are subjective phenomena; every evil and every good thing is a shadow which we cast" (III, 77).

But this is not the only, nor indeed the usual explanation which Emerson gives for the appearance and dependence of nature. "It is a sufficient account of that Appearance we call the World, that God will teach a human mind, and so makes it the receiver of a certain number of congruent sensations, which we call sun and moon, man and woman, house and trade" (I, 52). Indeed it is the purpose of Emerson's first little book on Nature to discover back of Nature the universal soul which produces it. "Spirit is the Creator. Spirit hath life in itself. And man in all ages and countries embodies it in his language as the Father" (I, 33). "Through all its kingdoms, to the suburbs and outskirts of things, it is faithful to the cause whence it had its origin. It always speaks of Spirit. It suggests the absolute. It is a perpetual effect. It is a great shadow pointing always to the sun behind us" (I, 65).

Thus it is not to the Fichtean side that Emerson inclines. Cabot says he had read Berkeley "in early youth," (p. 291); and he gives a letter to Margaret Fuller in which Emerson writes of "remembering the joy with which in my boyhood I caught the first hint of the Berkeleyan philosophy, and which I certainly never lost sight of afterwards." [77] But beyond this prejudice of his reading, we are forced to judge Emerson in this regard in the light of his natural attitude of mind. It has often been noted that it is largely a matter of temperament that one man holds to one system of philosophy and another to another. Certainly Idealism was a necessity to one of Emerson's nature, and just as certainly that form of Idealism which swamped the universal in the individual ego was impossible to him. His pages are full of the expression of his sense of the unimportance of his individual self in the great scheme of things. At times his statement of this seemingly contradictory point of view is characteristically extreme. "Nothing is of us. All is of God. The individual is always mistaken" (III, 71). But for the most part he has a less impassioned argument to offer. "A little consideration of what takes place around us every day would show us that a higher law than that of our will regulates events" (II, 132). "As with events, so with thoughts. When I watch that flowing river, which, out of regions I see not, pours for a season its streams into me, I see that I am a pensioner; not a cause but a surprised spectator of this ethereal water; that I desire and look up and put myself in the attitude of reception, but from some alien energy the visions come" (II, 252).

This contradiction must be resolved before we can go further. If the individual soul creates what it observes, and "God is but one of its ideas," then it is not "from some alien energy the visions come." That both of these are misstatements because overstatements, is patent. No one who reads him will think of taking it as Emerson's actual belief either that God—the real God—is no more than an idea of man, or that the source of things is "alien" to the observer. Let this most undeniable instance of the unreality of his contradictions speak for many more. Emerson, as I said before, is not to be read too literally. Moreover, we have exaggerated his disconnectedness; many of his statements are softened wonderfully when they are read in the tone of the essay in which they occur. And so perhaps the best way to allow Emerson to solve this seeming contradiction is to quote him while he makes it again and in the same breath. "It [the individual soul] feels that the grass grows and

---

[77] *A Memoir of Ralph Waldo Emerson*, vol. II, p. 478.

the stone falls by a law inferior to, and dependent on, its nature." And immediately the explanation follows: "Behold, it saith, I am born into the great, the universal mind. . . . I am somehow receptive of the great soul, and thereby do I overlook the sun and the stars and feel them to be the fair accidents and effects which change and pass. More and more the surges of everlasting nature enter into me, and I become public and human in my regards and actions. So come I to live in thoughts and act with energies which are immortal. Thus . . . man will come to see that the world is the perennial miracle which the soul worketh" (II, 277).

This, then, is the easy explanation. To say that the individual soul creates its objects and to say that God creates them is to say one and the same thing. "There is one mind common to all individual men. . . . Who hath access to this universal mind is party to all that is or can be done, for this is the only and sovereign agent. . . . Of this universal mind each individual man is one more *incarnation,* all its properties consist in him" (II, 9, 10). It was this extreme expression of pantheism which brought such ridicule upon Emerson at the outset of his career. "I am a transparent eyeball; I am nothing; I see all; the currents of the Universal Being circulate through me; I am part and parcel of God" (I, 16).

But Emerson soon perceived a danger in this point of view. The individual who is "part and parcel of God" is no individual at all; and at certain moments Emerson, like all the rest of us, felt his world of individual persons and things disappearing in an all-absorbing Totality. "I wish to speak with all respect of persons, but . . . they melt so fast into each other it needs an effort to treat them as individuals. . . . But this is flat rebellion. Nature will not be Buddhist. . . . She will not remain orbed in a thought but rushes into persons" (III, 224).

This brings us to the next and most important stage in Emerson's thinking. We have on the one hand "that overpowering reality," "that Unity, that Over-Soul, within which every man's particular being is contained and made one with all other" (II, 252), and to counterbalance this we have the statement that Nature "rushes into persons." Moreover, that these "persons" have the power of choice either to break the laws of Nature or to surrender themselves to the Universal Being is as fundamental a belief with Emerson as is the existence of that "Eternal One" which, by being so, seems to preclude all independent individuality. Indeed, if reduced to a dilemma between his idealism and his belief in the freedom and integrity of the individual, Emerson would, I think, have held to the latter.

> "For He that ruleth high and wise,
>   Nor pauseth in his plan,
> Will take the sun out of the skies
>   Ere freedom out of man" (IX, 174).

It becomes his problem henceforth, as it is that of all Idealism, to give a reality, a certain degree of independence and initiative, to the individuals who live in a world of universal spirit. How he attempts to reconcile these opposing points of view we shall consider in the following chapter.

But granting for the present that there is no final contradiction here, there is still a new difficulty in deciding how nature gets its permanence by its dependence upon the laws of mind. For if we once cease to be part of the spirit which is the cause of nature, our perception of nature must cease also; by this arrangement the evil-minded man would needs be blind and insensible, whereas his perception of nature is as good as that of the most virtuous.[78] This is a trivial objection, and one which Emerson never explained nor even noted, but it seems to me a necessary link in an attempt to give some completeness to his scheme. A suggestion of what his answer would have been is given, however, in a note in Emerson's Journal for June, 1835:

> "Our compound nature differences us from God, but our reason [79] is not to be distinguished from the Divine Essence. . . . It [the Divine Essence] is in all men, even the worst, and constitutes them men. In bad men it is dormant, in the good efficient: but it is perfect and identical in all, underneath the peculiarities, the vices, and the errors of the individual."

This is to say, by implication at least, that man has a three-fold nature,— a mere sensory organism which as a part of nature never loses hold of the reality of which it is only an effect, like the lower forms from which it was evolved; above this and springing from it, so to speak, into a certain independence of thought and action, comes this "mediating" faculty, the understanding; and finally, ready to surrender its freedom and return to the great reality from which it thus remotely came, is the reason.

---

[78] Carlyle, with more of an impulsive snatching at a truth and less calm clear-sightedness than Emerson, is led astray at this very point. In *Heroes and Hero-Worship* he contends that "a thoroughly immoral man could not know anything" (Edition in Longman's *English Classics*, p. 104).

[79] Under the immediate influence of Coleridge, Emerson is here distinguishing the reason from the understanding, which latter is the "executive faculty, the hand of the mind," which "mediates between the soul and inert matter," and "works in time and space." But this, written before his first independent venture in Transcendentalism proper, is merely an echo of German idealism, and does not bear the stamp of his own thinking. He continues, however, with this point of view, and gradually makes it his own.

But in all three of these developments, the great laws of nature continue their sway, and thus are we allied at every stage to that from which we came. "The next lesson taught is the continuation of the inflexible law of matter into the subtile kingdom of will and thought. . . . It is a short sight to limit our faith in laws to those of gravity, of chemistry, of botany, and so forth. Those laws do not stop where our eyes lose sight of them" (VI, 209).

These physical laws which extend their sway "into the subtile kingdom of will and thought" must be, of course, in their last analysis, the laws of spirit, and hence must be essentially *moral*. At the centre of being is that "moral force" of which "all force is the shadow or symbol" (III, 111). In saying that Discipline may be the Final Cause of the Universe, Emerson states this principle at the outset. From "Commodity" (that a man may be fed and in consequence that he may work)—to Beauty ("a nobler want of man")—to Language (nature "the symbol of spirit")—to Discipline, both of the Understanding and of the Reason (by which "the world becomes at last only a realized will" and all things become moral and "in their boundless changes have an unceasing reference to spiritual nature"—Emerson traces the uses of nature in that first wonderful rhapsody which announced the whole gospel of Transcendentalism. The uses of nature are ultimately moral because they culminate in this spiritual instruction of man, and "the secret of the illusoriness is the necessity of a succession of moods or objects" (III, 58). "The moral law lies at the centre of nature and radiates to the circumference. It is the pith and marrow of every substance, every relation, and every process" (I, 47). That "the laws of nature are laws of mind" is then a dual fact; first, because spirit is the source from which nature and its laws originally proceeded, and, second, because the evolution of Nature back to spirit produces in its progress the individual human minds. That man is the "result and interpreter of nature" means that he is the result of this great process, and the interpreter of it as nature. To state these laws in order would give us then the main points of Emerson's philosophy. He himself does not enumerate them, but they might be arranged somewhat in this order:

The first is the law of *Permanence,* by which we see that nature is not accidental, but a regular and orderly system, having its series of inviolable laws.

The second is the law of *Correspondence,* which shows that the laws of Nature are really laws of spirit, that is, of the individual mind.

The third is *Universality,* by which we know that the laws of my spirit are no other than the laws of all spirit, and that therefore I am part of "the great, the universal mind," which is "common to all men" and which "constitutes them men."

The fourth is *Progress,* which means that man is the "result" as well as the "interpreter" of nature. Here the individual emerges, asserting his claim to independence; and he does so by "losing hold" of this centrality. He evolves on a tangent, so to speak, and knows nature from which he came, but not God, who caused it.

And last there is the *Moral Law,* which underlies all these, and which shows that after all it is God at work, who must educate man through freedom. By this law, all nature exists for the education or "discipline" of man. Finally he returns, through self-surrender, to the great spirit from which he deviated.

CHAPTER IV.

The Philosophy of Emerson (*continued*): The Theories of Evolution and Emanation.

In spite of the patronizing tolerance in which it is usually held, the
course of Emerson's thought, as we have just outlined it, would seem to
one studying it sympathetically a fairly adequate putting together of
various phases of Idealism, and a reasonably consistent reading of them
as the main elements of a connected philosophy, if it were not for the
central contradiction which has been reserved for discussion in this chapter. This seems a modest claim enough to make for it; for the contradiction is as fatal as one could very well be. Let us state once more, in
Emerson's own words, this fundamental difficulty, and then proceed at
once to his answer. "In the divine order, Intellect is primary, Nature
secondary; it is the memory of the mind. That which once existed in
the intellect as pure law has now taken body as Nature" (I, 188). But
Nature "will not remain orbed in a thought, but rushes into persons"
(III, 225), and "When we break the laws, we lose our hold on the central reality" (VI, 305). The question is at once before us: How does
that which is "never a cause but a perpetual effect" produce those "persons" who have the fatal ability to lose hold of the central reality?

One who reads Emerson with the least care can hardly fail to notice
that this contradiction, like so many others in the history of philosophy,
is due primarily to a careless and inconsistent use of terms. We must
therefore pause at the very outset to make a fundamental distinction in
Emerson's use of the term "Nature."

In the introduction to his little book on Nature Emerson says: "I
shall use the word in both senses;—in its common and in its philosophical
import. In inquiries so general as the present one, the inaccuracy is not
material; no confusion of thought will occur" (I, 11). In the "philosophical" sense Emerson considers Nature as meaning "all that is separate from us, all which Philosophy distinguishes as the *Not Me,*—all
other men and my own body," but he still means to distinguish it from
Soul. But while he does distinguish it from the individual soul which
interprets this great reality as nature, he is not always careful to distinguish between this interpretation of ours, and the great unknown
reality of which it is the interpretation; and so, in one breath he may

speak of Nature as illusion, phenomenon, a "perpetual effect," whose laws are therefore wholly dependent on the laws of mind, and in the next moment, by a simple metonymy, he may continue to speak of "Nature" while he is clearly referring to the cause behind it.[80]

The confusion in Emerson's mind seems to have arisen from his endeavor to equate an inherited idealism, to which his adherence was largely emotional, with a theory of evolution which more and more forced itself upon him in his attempt to take account of an individual whose impulses proceed from within himself. Though he never wholly relinquished his belief that "nature proceeds from above," a growing belief in evolution may be traced throughout his work,—a belief so hostile to his earlier idealism that it finally forced him unconsciously to himself completely away from his earlier position. Let us trace briefly the growth of Emerson's belief in evolution, and see how it affected his answer to the problem of how a real individual may exist in a world of universal spirit. For it is his answer to this problem, which even Hegel sought in vain to solve, which gives to Emerson his real significance.

In his book, *Nature*, in 1836,—in spite of the many times that the claim has been made for it,—there is no suggestion of evolution beyond a "somewhat progressive"; nature is merely a "symbol" or "shadow" of spirit, a remoter and inferior incarnation of God, because an incarnation "in the unconscious"; it is nothing of itself, and does not work back to higher things; "a fact is merely the end or last issue of spirit" (I, 40). The famous verse ending,

> "And striving to be man, the worm
> Mounts through all the spires of form,"

prefixed to the essay as we now have it, did not appear till the second edition, in 1849; the motto which was prefixed to the edition of 1836 was from Plotinus, and merely to the effect that "Nature is but an image or imitation of wisdom,"—a more appropriate text for the book which follows. In this earliest work of Emerson's there is suggested by the fields and woods only "an occult relation between man and the vegetable" (I, 16); his later problem is, How is this occult relation to be accounted for?

It is on account of a certain instinctive anticipation of his later thinking, however, that Emerson, in *Nature*, is not wholly satisfied with Idealism as he finds it. It answers the question "What is matter?" but

---

[80] It would have been a great gain to clearness if Emerson had capitalized the word "Nature" when he meant to use it in this latter sense; but his use of capitals is wholly indiscriminate, not only as regards the word "Nature," but even in his use of the words "Spirit," "Soul," and "Mind."

not "Whence is it?" nor "Whereto?" (I, 66). "This theory makes nature foreign to me, and does not account for that consanguinity which we acknowledge to it"; he would leave it, therefore, "merely as a useful introductory hypothesis, serving to apprise us of the eternal distinction between the soul and the world" (I, 67).

We may fairly say, then, that *Nature* marks the first stage of Emerson's thinking, in which the individual is "part and parcel of God," God is pure spirit in the real sense of the term, having a definite purpose and hence a certain infinite intelligence and will, and the world, so far as we are concerned, is an illusion which God is using for the education of those individuals who after all are not individuals at all.

The assertion of the claims of the individual self against this overpowering reality was a necessity of Emerson's New England training, as it was of all western civilization. In philosophy, Emerson undoubtedly found it first in Plato. But it was almost immediately after his publishing of *Nature,* that is, toward the close of the year 1836, that he seems to have come under the influence of Lamarck, and we find his first advance beyond that "occult relation between animals and man" which he felt as early as 1832 (Cabot, vol. II, p. 710), and which was as far as he had gone up to this time. I quote from Emerson's lecture on "The Humanity of Science," abstracted "as nearly as possible in his own words," by Mr. Cabot:

"Lamarck finds a monad of organic life common to every animal, and becoming a worm, a mastiff, or a man, according to circumstances. He says to the caterpillar, How dost thou, brother? Please God, you shall yet be a philosopher. And the instinct finds no obstacle in the objects. . . . Step by step we are apprised of another fact, namely, the humanity of that spirit in which Nature works; that all proceeds from a mind congenial with ours." (*A Memoir of Ralph Waldo Emerson,* vol. II, p. 725.)

But we must know nature in its very essence, or else there is something in the universe essentially apart from us. So Emerson's next step is the establishment of the actuality of the kinship of man to external nature. Again I quote from Mr. Cabot's careful analysis, and this time from the lectures on "Human Culture" given during the following winter (1837-38):

"Man drinks of that nature whose property it is to be *Cause.* With the first surge of that ocean he affirms, *I am.* Only Cause can say I. But as soon as he has uttered this word he transfers this *me* from that which it really is to the frontier region of effects, to his body and its appurtenances, to place and time. Yet is he continually wooed to abstract himself from effects and dwell with causes: to ascend into the region of law. Few men enter it, but all men belong there." (*Ib.,* vol. II, p. 734).

This is the most impossible of compromises, and some sort of explanation was an immediate necessity. Man cannot "belong" in one kind of existence and "be" in another. And so Emerson makes the distinction the following year that "man is related by his form to the world about him; by his soul to the universe,—passing through what a scale, from reptile sympathies to enthusiasm and ecstasy" (*Ib.*, p. 737). This is certainly not explanation, for it leaves an impossible dualism in the nature of man.

Emerson does little to solve this difficulty in his next series (1839-40): "Nothing but God is self-dependent. Man is powerful only by the multitude of his affinities. Our being is a reproduction of all the past. . . . The great Cause is alive, is life itself" (*Ib.*, p. 743). But this Hegelian attitude of mind was out of Emerson's range, and he falls back with a certain sense of security, as he does all through his life, on his older and surer "intuitions"; "What are we all but the instant manifestation of the Divine energy? . . . A man is not a man who does not yet draw on the universal and eternal soul" (*Ib.*, p. 746).

This brings us to the year 1841, in which appeared the remarkable address on the "Method of Nature," and the First Series of the Essays, in which are contained some of Emerson's most final suggestions of theory; so that we may consider from this point on, in what form the problem now appealed to him, and what was the logical if not the chronological development of his answer.[81]

By idealism pure and simple, as the dilemma now appeared to the mind of Emerson, we must remain mere "ideas," whereas if we were a

---

[81] The Journals give us little to add and nothing to subtract from this statement of the development of Emerson's thinking through these critical years. The very language of the lectures may be found under dates closely corresponding, and I find nothing of real significance which is not stated or implied in the lectures. In 1836 Emerson is saying, "Man is the point wherein matter and spirit meet and marry" (Journals, IV, p. 78). He is of course more natural and explicit in wrestling with his problem in the soliloquy of the Journal than in his public utterances, though no more sincere and direct. In the Journal from which I have just quoted he writes (page 247): "I see my being imbedded in Universal Mind. . . . I believe in Unity but behold two." It is thus that the problem appeared to him before the principle of evolution became a vital thing with him. He feels a "sympathy with nature" but finds "little access." At certain moments he knows that he exists "directly from God," and then he becomes "a surprised spectator"; and he asks pathetically, "Can't I see the universe without a contradiction?" Next he finds that beasts are "wholly immersed in the apparent," that a "common soul broods over them, they are never individual as man is" (Journals, IV, p. 381). Beyond this evidence that Emerson was *reasoning* and not simply grappling with mystical intuitions, the Journals for the years 1836-1841 give us nothing that need detain us.

product of the evolving reality itself the unity of this great reality would be imperiled. Was there any compromise possible? Could there be any bridge between these two positions?

The first reconciliation which presented itself was the Emanation theory as he found it in Neo-Platonism. But on this he was forced to put a highly spiritualistic interpretation of his own. For Emerson was still striving to hold to the spiritual actuality of the source of things and to a certain independent finality in the individuals produced by this eternal process. Naturally he could find in Plotinus little encouragement beyond the mere idea of a perpetual emanation and return. But would it not be a sufficient account alike of the individual and the universal, if the world were conceived as an efflux of spirit, which, embodied for a time as nature, finally works back to spirit again? Emerson's statement of this is of course highly symbolic:

"It is a steep stair down from the essence of Intellect pure to thoughts and intellections. As the sun is conceived to have made our system by hurling out from itself the outer rings of diffuse ether which slowly condensed into earths and moons, by a higher force of the same law the mind detaches minds, and a mind detaches thoughts or intellections. These again all mimic in their sphericity the first mind, and share its power" (XII, 16).

Now it is impossible from the very nature of things that these "emanations," if they are of the same nature as God, could ever become "detached." Indeed, the very word "detach" is meaningless when applied to mind. Furthermore, if these minds are like the original mind and "share its power," they should be able to give to their "thoughts or intellections" another independent existence, which it is obvious we can not do; nor would we speak in the language of space and time if the original mind did not. If we are of the same nature as God, we cannot receive the impressions he gives us and body them forth as a physical universe, unless he himself does so; and what becomes of Transcendentalism if space and time are the same to God as they seem to us?

When Emerson says, "Nature is the incarnation of a thought and turns to thought again" (III, 187), he still knows very well that a thought cannot be incarnated; that if it were the thought of anyone, even of God, it could have no separate existence, could by no means evolve or *turn* to anything. We cannot conceive of God as sowing ideas and reaping from them a spiritual substance. If nature were no more than the thought of spirit, we would be likewise no more than parts of speech— so many nouns in the grammar of God—and our subjective independence would be as hopelessly lost as ever.

Time and again Emerson's Idealism does drive him to confess this very point of view, at least so far as the lower orders of nature are concerned. Thus he says boldly, "These metals and animals . . . are words of God and as fugitive as other words" (II, 293). But while it is well enough to say that all the rest of creation is the thinking of God, Emerson cannot seriously consider himself as the mere thought of some Being. How could he become so far separate from the Eternal One as to put an interpretation upon him or upon his other "ideas"? This drives him to the impossible explanation:

"Whilst we converse with truths as thoughts, they exist also as plastic forces; as the soul of a man, the soul of a plant, the genius or constitution of any part of nature, which makes it what it is. The thought which was in the world, part and parcel of the world, has disengaged itself and taken an independent existence" (XII, 5).

But in feeling this need for thoughts which are more than thoughts,—which in being "plastic forces" are not thoughts at all,— Emerson was driven from his theory of emanation to a theory of evolution which precluded the emanation idea. Upon this he was still able to put a thoroughly idealistic interpretation; but that his gradual formation and acceptance of this theory did modify the type of idealism with which he started, there can be no doubt. In his first book, *Nature*, in 1836, Emerson feels that the evidence of our own being is "perfect" but that the world "is a divine dream, from which we may presently awake to the glories and certainties of day" (I, 66); in the essay on "Illusions," published in the *Conduct of Life*, in 1860, he speaks of our pretension of selfhood as "fading with the rest," and finds "that in the endless striving and ascents, the metamorphosis is entire" (VI, 303). This is the main change,—from a purely idealistic interpretation of the world as illusion to an attempt to account for the presence of the individual by an evolution where "the metamorphosis is entire."

Much has been said of Emerson's belief in evolution, as being an anticipation of the work of Darwin. Nothing could be further from the obvious facts than this. Except that he stood nearer to the day of scientific demonstration and had in consequence a slight leaning at times toward the scientific manner, there is nothing in Emerson which advances beyond the conclusions reached by Herder,—not to remark again that the belief in evolution is as old as recorded thought.[82] Though he probably had not read the writings of Herder or Oken, Emerson had some

[82] "The waters contained a germ from which everything else sprang forth" says the Rig-Veda, and with many such suggestions as this Emerson was unquestionably familiar.

preparation for the reception of ideas similar to theirs.[83] But no direct influence or indebtedness is necessary here. Such ideas as these are always in the air for some time before the actual Darwin verifies them, and as Emerson himself remarks, the poet is always the first to feel them, though any man might easily anticipate the discovery. "Because the history of nature is charactered in his brain, therefore is he the prophet and discoverer of her secrets. Every known fact in natural science was divined by the presentiment of somebody, before it was actually verified" (III, 176). Emerson's remained a poetic or at best a purely metaphysical anticipation of the fact of evolution, and so he stands wholly apart from all that constitutes the real significance of Darwin. Even after the theory had been established, it is in the same attitude that he looks back upon it. "Science was false by being unpoetical. It assumed to explain a reptile or mollusk, and isolated it,—which is hunting for life in graveyards. Reptile or mollusk or man or angel only exist in system, in relation. The metaphysician, the poet, only sees each animal form as an inevitable step in the path of the creating mind" (VIII, 15).

---

[83] See Dr. Edward Waldo Emerson's Biographical Sketch in the Centenary Edition (vol. I, pp. xxvi-xxx).

CHAPTER V.

The Philosophy of Emerson (*continued*): The Identity of Subject and Object.

It would seem that in accepting the doctrine of evolution Emerson would scarcely have been able to remain a mystic; and indeed it is often said that he wrote sometimes as a mystic and sometimes not. I think this is a mistake. In the fundamental principles of mysticism he never wavered.[84] However much he wrestled with his problem, and arrived stage by stage at his conclusions through definite processes of the "understanding," he still felt a religious exaltation in the moments of his deepest insights, and this kept him firm in his belief in intuition and hence in the first-hand or original character of his perceptions. "When we are exalted by ideas," he says boldly, "we do not owe this to Plato, but to the idea, to which also Plato was debter" (IV, 24).[85] In like manner, however much Emerson may have been led either directly or through Coleridge toward the "Identitäts" system of Schelling, which he is now about to offer as his final solution of the central problem of metaphysics, he arrived at his results from an entirely different point of approach, and it is this, rather than the actual results which he announces, that gives to his thinking its peculiar interest and value. "Do not teach me out of Schelling," he exclaims in his Journal, "and I shall find it all out for myself." Let us see, therefore, by what process Emerson seems to have gone forward in his thinking from the point at which we left it in the last chapter to the "Identity" theory toward which he was constantly inclining.

Omitting the starting-point of the existence of spirit before its expression of itself as nature, since this expression was always a necessity of

---

[84] To state the four propositions of mystical faith as given by Mr. Inge in his *Christian Mysticism* (pages 6, 7), is to state four of the most fundamental tenets in Emerson's philosophy. These are: (1) The soul (as well as the body) can see and perceive; (2) Man in order to know God must be a partaker of the divine nature; (3) "Without holiness no man may see the Lord"; and (4) The true hierophant of the mysteries of God, is love. Besides these there are many minor tenets in Mysticism as Mr. Inge explains it which are fundamental facts with Emerson, as that "Evil has no separate existence" (page 25).

[85] Mysticism has no genealogy," says Vaughan in his *Hours with the Mystics*, but "grows spontaneously in a certain temperament of mind."

its existence and could never have had an actual beginning in time, we have a logical priority which does not interfere with an ontological explanation more in accord with the obvious facts of the great evolution. We have the universal spirit as a developing or evolving reality, whose expression of itself in the successive states a, b, c, we interpret as inorganic matter, the plant creation, the animal creation; we have no longer a mere Being, self-sufficient and passive, whose "thoughts" take body as nature and then of their own initiative turn to thought again. This becomes at once a mere figure of speech by which the priority of mind stands only for the reality of spirit; and nature, in being the perpetual and neccessary and to us explanatory effect, is no more than our interpretation of the very essence of spirit. To know the Universal spirit, therefore, we must study nature in its long progress from inorganic matter up to man; and thus we shall be able to write, at least in part, a "Natural History of Intellect." This is what Emerson means when he says, "I believe in the existence of the material world as the expression of the spiritual or real, and in the impenetrable mystery which hides (and hides through absolute transparency) the mental nature, I await the insight which our advancing knowledge of material laws shall furnish" (XII, 5; and X, 74).[86]

Nature, as we come to know it in our study of Geology, is a "manifestation of God in the unconscious," or, as we must now interpret it, a manifestation of God before he attained to consciousness. But in his very nature, in the atoms, so to speak, of his original existence was an "outward impulse" (to borrow the word of Alexander Bain),—a "desire" to be other,—and of this desire in its constant realization, all nature and all human history is the continuous record.

"We can point nowhere to anything final, but tendency appears on all hands; planet, system, constellation, total nature is growing like a field of maize in July; is becoming somewhat else; is in rapid metamorphosis. The embryo does not more strive to be man, than yonder burr of light we call a nebula tends to be a ring, a comet, a globe, and parent of new stars" (I, 194).

But having made, in his own mind, a start in this direction, it seems to me that Emerson felt a great danger ahead of him. If consciousness was after all only a late step in the evolution of God, what is to save us from the terrible clutches of Materialism?—for until God attained to consciousness, he could not be Spirit at all in any proper sense of the term. I think this half-realized dread is the psychological explanation of Emerson's constant insistence upon his extreme statements of Idealism even

---

[86] The statement is identical in both passages.

after he had attained his later position. Though he claims to have no
fear of this frightful word (II, 285), yet it alone causes him to lose con-
trol of himself. "The physicians say they are not materialists; but they
are:—Spirit is matter reduced to an extreme thinness: O *so* thin!— . . .
I see not, if one be once caught in this trap of so-called sciences,
any escape for the man from the links of the chain of physical necessity.
Given such an embryo, such a history must follow. On this platform one
lives in a sty of sensualism, and would soon come to suicide" (III, 56,
57). This is strangely unlike Emerson's usual calm tone.

But our being caught in the chain of physical necessity results "from
looking too much at one condition of nature, namely Motion" (III, 186).
"The astronomers said, 'Give us matter and a little motion and we will
construct the universe. It is not enough that we should have matter, we
must also have a single impulse, one shove to launch the mass and generate the harmony of the centrifugal and centripetal forces.' . . . Nature,
meanwhile, had . . . bestowed the impulse and the balls rolled. . . .
That famous aboriginal push propagates itself through all the balls of
the systems and through every atom of every ball: through all the races
of creatures, and through the history and performances of every individual" (III, 176, 177).

Yet in attributing this impulse to the "primordial atom" Emerson
himself reads almost like a materialist; when he speaks of "the genetical
atom of which both [plants and animals] are composed" (XII, 212), it
is hard to remember what a visionary dreamer he was. But in his very
use of the word "atoms" Emerson is only trying to make us feel the absolute necessity and completeness of spirit's expression of itself in the
guise of nature,—the actual identity of the two. "The next step in the
series is the equivalence of the soul to nature" (VIII, 209). It is therefore only two instances of the same law that "atom draws to atom
throughout nature, and truth to truth throughout spirit" (VIII, 211),
since "There is a kind of latent omniscience not only in every man but in
every particle" (X, 177) ; or as he puts it in the verse introductory to his
last essay on Nature,

"Self-kindled every atom glows" (III, 161).

The atom which is "self-kindled" is a spiritual being; or at least, to Emerson it seemed so.[86a]

Since spirit is not to be separated from its expression of itself as

---

[86a] Too little has been made of Emerson's obvious sympathy with and indebtedness to Leibnitz. The strong individualism of this philosopher offered the same
comfort to Emerson that it did to Schleiermacher; but the American's greater
love of freedom led him much further in this direction.

nature, this expression must be not only complete but perpetual. "We can never surprise nature in a corner; never find the end of a thread; never tell where to set the first stone. The bird hastens to lay her egg; the egg hastens to be a bird. The wholeness we admire in the order of the world is the result of infinite distribution . . . its permanence is perpetual inchoation. Every natural fact is an emanation, and that from which it emanates is an emanation also, and from every emanation is a new emanation." And then follows the important first step in the great evolution: "In all animal and vegetable forms, the physiologist concedes that no chemistry, no mechanics, can account for the facts, but a mysterious principle of life must be assumed, which not only inhabits the organ but makes the organ" (I, 190).

The significance of this passage for a correct understanding of Emerson's thought is far-reaching. If the evolution of inorganic nature into man is a real evolution, there must creep in no dualism, no parallelism, between nature and mind. We find certain parts of inorganic nature suddenly and inexplicably equipped with a new principle—life. In like manner we must consider consciousness. With Emerson there is no more of a dualism between mind and matter than there is between life and matter; each is a new principle, a new step in the evolution of the spiritual substance.

"It is a long way from granite to the oyster; farther yet to Plato and the preaching of the immortality of the soul. Yet all must come, as surely as the first atom has two sides. . . . A little water made to rotate in a cup explains the formation of the simpler shells; the addition of matter from year to year arrives at last at the most complex forms; and yet so poor is nature with all her craft, that from the beginning to the end of the universe she has but one stuff,—but one stuff with its two ends, to serve up all her dream-like variety. Compound it how she will, star, sand, fire, water, tree, man, it is still one stuff, and betrays the same properties" (III, 173, 174).

There is, then, no creation of anything really new,—no transcendence of the laws of inorganic nature by the laws of life, or of consciousness, or of will. "Nature is always consistent, though she feigns to contravene her own laws. She keeps her laws, and seems to transcend them" (Ib.). "Intellect and morals appear only the material forces on a higher plane. The laws of material nature run up into the invisible world of the mind" (X, 74).

In being compelled to postulate "a deeper cause, as yet far from being conscious" (II, 72), Emerson was certainly relinquishing the pure idealism with which he started. Yet there was no escape for him. In

choosing between the theories of emanation and of evolution he was reduced to a choice between two equally unsatisfactory alternatives: that
God, as a conscious spirit, creates a world of appearance, which eternally
works back into real being again; or that God is impersonal, the very
essence of things, and reaches his culmination in man. The first of these
is God with a fictitious universe, the freedom of the individual being a
part of the illusion; the second is a world with a fictitious God.

Of course neither of these could be Emerson's final view of things.
His task must be to find a common ground alike for spirit and for nature.
The great reality must continue to be spirit in its very essence; but if it
is to account for this real world it must be not only spirit but more than
spirit; nature must be as real an expression of it as spirit itself.

And this leads to the inevitable result of trying to take account of
both truths at once, of "the unity of cause and the variety of appearance"; we must conclude that Spirit, as well as nature, is essentially an
interpretation of our own. Just as we are driven from Materialism by
the need to take account of the appearance of something forever different
from matter, so we are driven from the deeper but still inadequate conception of evolving spirit, in order to give any reality or independence to
the individual. Aud thus is Emerson driven to his final theory of the
identity of subject and object in "a substance older and deeper than either
mind or matter" (VIII, 15).

There are three great dangers which we are apt to fall into in our
attempt to define the nature of this ultimate reality: we may make of it
a mere logical abstraction, and in our desire not to deprive nature and
spirit of their mutual relation and efficiency, we may land in a dualism
with only a theoretical common ground of being; or wishing to escape
this alternative and preserve at all costs the unity of the "Eternal One,"
we may fall into a worse mistake and sink both world and spirit in this
immovable, overpowering Reality; or finally, hoping to avoid both of
these dangers, wishing to gain both unity and potency for the underlying
substance and reality for both nature and mind, we may have proposed
only a *tertium quid,* which is no solution of the great problem at all. To
translate these three dangers to be avoided into three propositions to be
established, we must find this Reality to be essentially One, yet to include
in itself both spirit and nature, and to have therefore a reality as great as
theirs and a potency as effective in producing a world of actual spirit and
of actual nature;—so that we may justly call this substance, according to
our viewpoint, the "All-dissolving Unity," the "underlying Reality," or
the "Great First Cause."

The insistence upon unity always seems at first to be bought at the expense of reality. Emerson insists constantly upon both sides of the great dilemma, but he stands before the real problem of the One and the Many as hopeless as every greater philosopher since the mighty Greeks. But that this unity is an eternal fact is with Emerson perhaps the most fundamental of all truths. "All the universe over there is but one thing, this old Two-Face, creator-creature, mind-matter, right-wrong, of which any proposition may be affirmed or denied" (III, 233). But no supplying of hyphens can give a real unity to contradictory elements,—nor any such echoes of past philosophers as that "Nature is one thing and the other thing in the same moment" (III, 225), or that "cause and effect are two sides of one fact" (II, 293). But Emerson does not often offend in this way. The unity so strongly insisted upon is an "all-dissolving unity" (VIII, 212); it has in itself the very essence of both nature and spirit, for "it is impossible that the creative power should exclude itself" (III, 58). So while it is a higher reality than spirit,—something from which this narrow and restricted *personal* spirit could emanate,—it is not less real than spirit, indeed does not cease to be spirit; and as spirit Emerson refers to it immediately after saying that "in our more correct writings we give to this generalization the name of Being, and thereby confess that we have arrived as far as we can go" (III, 75). In like manner, as the unfolding of the life of this great Reality is shown in the evolution of nature, it is therefore at the same time Nature itself, and with a consistency which seems almost perversity, Emerson calls it by this name even while insisting upon its underlying unity and ultimately spiritual essence.

We see, then, that this search after unity, which is the "noble rage" of all philosophers, was supplemented in Emerson by the instincts of the man of sense who can never content himself with an ideal unity or a metaphysical system perfect in logic but deficient in its power of ultimate conviction. Even in his most "transcendental" stage, in his book on *Nature,* he sets himself the philosophical standard which he never deserts. "Whenever a true theory appears, it will be its own evidence. Its test is, that it will explain all phenomena" (I, 10). If his theory of identity is to be of any service to Emerson, it must be because this Unity, this Reality, has in itself the power to produce this actual world of mind and matter,—its unity must be the "unity of cause" and its reality must account for the "variety of appearance." And so Emerson at last considers it. It is "the Efficient Nature, *natura naturans,* the quick cause before which all forms flee as the driven snow; itself secret, its works driven before it in flocks and multitudes . . . arriving at consummate results without a shock or leap" (III, 172).

In his calmer moments this figurative language disappears, and Emerson speaks as simply as he can: "Shall we describe this cause as that which works directly?" (III, 75). "The great and cressive self, rooted in absolute nature, supplants all relative existence" (III, 78). But we cannot help feeling, as he does, the utter inadequacy of all this. He seems to come nearer the truth when he speaks in symbols; and feeling this himself, it is notably characteristic of him that he at once attributes this same attitude to other men. With a most innocent lack of philosophic perspective, he remarks: "The baffled intellect must still kneel before this cause, which refuses to be named,—ineffable cause, which every fine genius has essayed to represent by some emphatic symbol, as Thales by water, Anaximenes by air, Anaxagoras by (Νοῦς) thought, Zoroaster by fire, Jesus and the moderns by love: and the metaphor of each has become a national religion" (III, 74).

But for Emerson himself the symbol was necessary not because of the uncertainty, but because by its very nature the ultimate Reality could not be adequately expressed in any other way. For if we content ourselves with calling it such names as Being or First Cause or the Eternal One we do not take account of its fulness and richness,—of the fact that "that central life is superior to creation," that "forever it labors to create a life and thought as large and excellent as itself, but in vain" (II, 297). And so when Emerson calls this Reality Spirit or Nature, he speaks no less symbolically than when he calls it Goodness (II, 289), or Wisdom (III, 188), or by any other name; for in including in itself all of these great principles it cannot be adequately called by the name of any one of them. We are reduced to the language which suggests, which half reveals, but which never really betrays its meaning to the understanding. We would fain escape this dealing with what is other than we in terms of ourselves,—but how can we? How can we picture spaceless objects or conceive of timeless events? No more can the understanding escape from its own categories; the reason conceives of a great Reality like to itself, but the understanding must needs name it Spirit;—or, in wilder attempt to express this essence of things, must call it by some fantastic or symbolic name, as Creative Love, or Impersonal Reason, or Truth, or Justice, or Ideal Beauty; but we speak still in terms of ourselves; and so long as we speak or interpret at all, there is no escape from this. But when the faculties of the mere mind are closed and the underlying Reality which is in us and sustains us in our very existence awakes to consciousness, then do we truly perceive, or rather, then does Reality perceive itself;—then does the worshipper become one with him whom he adores (II, 274),—then does God "commune with himself."

We may now see that Emerson's early statement, that the understanding is fallen,—does not comprehend,—but that "our reason is not to be distinguished from the Divine Essence" (Cabot, p. 246), is conventional, and is really no more than he may easily have found (and undoubtedly did find) in Coleridge. It is quite in Coleridge's manner, and lacks all sign of first-hand discovery. It has no philosophical influence upon his original work immediately following; and yet this sentence expresses the very utmost of his philosophical reach. Later, the rapt, inspirational tone in which he speaks shows that he is no longer attempting to solve problems, but that he is telling of things which to him are sacred. Knowing that he is foredoomed to failure in his attempt to utter that which is by its very nature unutterable, Emerson still attempts to say what this Reality is; and this seems to me his deepest thought concerning the great Problem:

"Meantime within man is the soul of the whole; the wise silence; the universal beauty, to which every part and particle is equally related; the eternal ONE. And this deep power in which we exist and whose beatitude is all accessible to us, is not only self-sufficing and perfect in every hour, but the act of seeing and the thing seen, the seer and the spectacle, the subject and the object, are one. We see the world piece by piece, as the sun, the moon, the animal, the tree; but the whole, of which these are shining parts, is the soul. . . . I dare not speak for it. . . . All goes to show that the soul in man is not an organ, but animates and exercises all the organs; is not a function . . . is not a faculty, but a light; is not the intellect or the will, but the master of the intellect and the will; is the background of our being, in which they lie,—an immensity not possessed and that cannot be possessed. . . . When it breathes through his intellect it is genius; when it breathes through his will, it is virtue; when it flows through his affection it is love. . . . It contradicts all experience. . . . It abolishes time and space. . . . The soul knows only the soul; the web of events is the flowing robe in which she is clothed" (II, 253-257).

And so that brilliant but mystical essay on the "Over-Soul" proceeds,—suggesting wonderful reaches of truth to those who have had experiences like Emerson's own,—suggesting nothing at all to the mass of men or the mere thinkers. But at the point of its approach to real originality and greatness, Emerson's thought rises out of the realm of Philosophy altogether and dwells in the pure region of Religion. At this point, therefore, we must leave our attempt to trace his philosophical development, and concern ourselves with that faculty, or rather condition of mind in which the New England Transcendentalists thought the "pure practical reason" asserted its claims:—"that blessed mood," as Wordsworth calls it in his "Tintern Abbey,"

"In which the burden of the mystery,
In which the heavy and the weary weight
Of all this unintelligible world
Is lightened:—that serene and blessed mood
In which the affections gently lead us on,—
Until, the breath of this corporeal frame,
And even the motion of our human blood,
Almost suspended, we are laid asleep
In body, and become a living soul:
While with an eye made quiet by the power
Of harmony, and the deep power of joy,   ·
We see into the life of things."

Our problem now becomes more technical and perhaps more tangible, though still dealing with elements forever somewhat vague, than the unraveling of Emerson's metaphysics has been—the chronicling of those glimmering suggestions of theory which were and were not his. What is really the meaning and significance of this belief in intuition? If it was a purely religious experience, superinduced by a certain exalted state of mind, is it to be dealt with as merely a pathological condition, and is that to negate wholly the religious implications which are derived from it?

CHAPTER VI.

THE EPISTEMOLOGICAL BASIS OF EMERSON'S PHILOSOPHY: THE THEORY
OF INTUITION.

Having attempted a general analysis of what we may term Emerson's metaphysics, we are in some position to consider that element of his system which, with even greater apologies, we must call his epistemology.

Emerson's belief in intuition was a logical deduction from his theory of identity. But it must be remembered that while the identity theory was a gradual growth in his mind, a belief in intuition was always at the very center of his system; that therefore the meaning he attaches to his faith in intuition will vary according to the stage he has arrived at philosophically in his theory of identity. I confess that this statement would have met with surprise and probably also with denial from Emerson himself, but I think it is true nevertheless.

The usual opinion regarding Emerson's belief in intuition is that it is simply the unexplained and unphilosophical assumption of all Mysticism, namely, that the soul perceives because it is a part of the great all-knowing Reality; or, as Emerson himself puts it, that the intellect's vision is "not like the vision of the eye, but is a union with the things known" (II, 304). This, so far as it goes, is a correct statement of Emerson's theory in every stage of its development, and, stated thus broadly, it is one which he never denies or contradicts. But again, stated thus broadly, nothing could be more hopeless of explanation than such a theory. By this "union," the Over-Soul not only fills but is the individual soul, just as the ocean tide fills and floods for a time the shallow brook flowing into it, and becomes one with it, and then retreats again, leaving the "brook," the individual mind, with only "a far-off memory." But this "influx of the Divine mind into our mind" (II, 263), is a "possession" which leaves no room for anything but itself, so that to say we perceive in these great moments is only another way of saying that "the Maker . . . casts his dread omniscience through us over things (Ib.); and yet, again, the individual mind must be something quite other than this universal spirit, for we are told that "we need only obey," that we have the power to "surrender" our wills, to "place" ourselves in the "stream of power and wisdom which animates all it floats," that we may "allow" the currents of the universal soul to flow unimpeded through our being; indeed we may recognize its presence as a "joy and exultation"; and to receive it is an act of "piety."

But Emerson's "intuition" continued to tell him that these things were so, however unaccountable they might be. That intuition was not to be explained by this first general statement of it he fully recognized; and through the year 1841, when his First Series of Essays was published, he continues to state the hopelessness of any attempt at explanation. In his address on "The Method of Nature" in that year, he writes: "But at last what has he to recite but the fact that there is a Life not to be described or known otherwise than by possession? What account has he to give of his essence more than *so it was to be?* . . . There is the incoming or the receding of God: that is all we can affirm; and we can show neither how nor why" (I, 195). And again, in the essay on "Self-Reliance," though recognizing the common origin of ourselves and of nature, he does not yet see how intuition is to be explained: "We denote this primary wisdom as Intuition, whilst all later teachings are tuitions. In that deep force, the last fact behind which analysis cannot go, all things find their common origin. For the sense of being which in calm hours rises, we know not how, in the soul, is not diverse from things, from space, from light, from time, from man, but one with them and proceeds obviously from the same source whence their life and being also proceed." For a moment we seem on the verge of an explanation. "We first share the life by which things exist and afterwards see them as appearances in nature and forget that we have shared their cause." But "if we ask whence this comes, if we seek to pry into the soul that causes, all philosophy is at fault. Its presence or its absence is all we can affirm" (II, 64, 65).

Because of Emerson's so constant insistence upon this merely mystical point of view, especially in his better known and more purely philosophical essays, it is commonly felt that he makes no advance upon it. Intuition remains a "pious reception," or at best a "glad and conspiring reception," an openness "of one side of our nature" to receive new truth; and farther than this, even Cabot says, "he did not attempt to go in the way of doctrine." [87] But though Mr. Cabot knew Emerson's writings so intimately, and his work under Emerson's own eye was always so wholly satisfactory to his master, yet there does seem to be more to say for Emerson's intuition theory than just this. In the Essays of the Second Series and in all his writings after 1844, the thought of an explanation was in Emerson's mind,—the growing desire to write a "Natural History of Intellect," which at last he tried—and failed—to do.

[87] *A Memoir of Ralph Waldo Emerson,* vol. I, p. 235.

It was not, it seems to me, the impossibility of explaining intuition so much as the very assurance it claimed for itself that led in Emerson's mind to the demand for a deeper account of it. Indeed, this positiveness of the intuition is its own negation; for if it may ever know wrongly, so that a later intuition may contradict or transcend it, then it may always know wrongly, and there is no test for it. Though Emerson will not admit this directly, yet we find him in his later essays becoming less assertive and more inquisitive regarding the ultimate nature of this perception of actuality; and as soon as he does this the conclusion becomes inevitable that the self-consciousness of the reason is a relative matter; that while indeed the soul could not perceive falsely, yet there must be certain conditions which clog and hinder its perfect vision; that it must not be separated too completely from the understanding, and from the processes of nature by which it is derived.

When Emerson came to consider that a deeper cause than spirit must be postulated as the ground of being, the explanation of intuition was at once possible though it seems not to have been immediately apparent to himself. If he could have accepted this new solution frankly and fully, and not have bound himself down (though of course with entire honesty) to a continued adherence to those earlier "intuitions" which he had unconsciously outgrown, there would be no confusion in following out his system to its close. But the religious, the supernatural side of intuition impressed him so deeply that he no sooner made a new "generalization" than he felt the need of stating, side by side with it, his belief in the old. It is this that makes his essays so baffling, that has led so many to feel the utter hopelessness of trying to find in them any order or consistency whatever.

From the very start Emerson taught that "Nature is the present expositor of the Divine mind," and can be wholly known to man since "its laws are laws of his own mind;" and hence he could say that "the ancient precept, 'Know thyself,' and the modern precept, 'Study nature,' become at last one maxim" (I, 88). But so long as he gave even a nominal adherence to the purely idealistic theory of the dependence of nature upon spirit, every door to a possible explanation of intuition was closed to him. That he felt this, and was about to make a new "generalization" appears plainly from his essay on "Circles," in what is perhaps the most significant sentence in his whole philosophy. "Fear not the new generalization. Does the fact look crass and material, threatening to degrade thy theory of spirit? Resist it not; it goes to refine and raise thy theory of matter just as much" (II, 285). Yet nowhere in the Second Series of Essays, where he is most concerned with giving the causes of things which before he had merely assumed, does he quite come to the point of the explanation of his chief difficulty. In the last essay on Nature, though here we find the balance wholly in favor of evolution and the identity of the soul with nature, he has only the tone of explanation, with no real advance, so far as intuition is concerned, beyond his first position:

"This guiding identity runs through all the surprises and contrasts of the piece, and characterizes every law. Man carried the world in his head, the whole astronomy and chemistry suspended in a thought. Because the history of nature is charactered in his brain, therefore is he the prophet and discoverer of her secrets" (III, 176).

In like manner, in the "Experience" essay, in the "Nominalist and Realist," and in the less frequent philosophical passages in the other essays of this series, he contents himself with proclaiming again the unlimited "extent" and "validity" of intuition, while he makes no clear statement as to the "origin" of our knowledge of things. But in the introductory essay to his next book, *Representative Men*, Emerson no longer hesitates to draw the inevitable conclusion:

"The possibility of interpretation lies in the identity of the observer with the observed. Each material thing has its celestial side; has its translation, through humanity, into the spiritual and necessary sphere where it plays a part as indestructible as any other. And to these, their ends, all things continually ascend. The gases gather to the solid firmament; the chemic lump arrives at the plant, and grows; arrives at the quadruped, and walks; arrives at the man, and thinks. But also the constituency determines the vote of the representative. He is not only representative, but participant. Like can be known only by like. The reason why he knows about them is that he is of them; he has just come out of nature, or from being a part of that thing" (IV, 16).

Now if there is indeed a final consistency in Emerson's thought, an underlying synthesis possible for even the main elements of it, it must lie in his final belief that the intuition is due not only to the spiritual essence of the "Reason," but also to the fact that the self-consciousness of the Reason is itself the result of the evolution of "Nature." In Emerson's first period the perception of the individual "reason" is due to some inexplicable union with the universal "Reason," followed by an even more incomprehensible severance from it; but by the coming in of the evolution theory a seemingly rational explanation of intuition becomes possible.

And yet, stripping it of its transcendental coloring, what is this but the merest realism? Nominally, intuition remains to the end an "angel-whispering,—which discomfits the conclusions of nations and of years" (III, 69); but in cold actuality "We define Genius to be a sensibility to all the impressions of the outer world" (X, 78), and genius, be it remembered, is the action of the soul when it "sees absolute truth" (I, 91).

According to Emerson, then, the common background of being rises in the lower animals to the point of instinct, which is "nature when it first becomes intelligent" (XII, 33), and "Inspiration," which is the visible working of intuition in man, "is only this power excited, breaking its silence" (XII, 32). Thus the instinct of animals, which is the same in kind as intuition in man, though lower in the stage of its development, is still "higher than the understanding" (I, 319). But this sharing of the common nature is all there is to the plant or animal, for only the Intellect "emancipates the individual, for infinite good and also for infinite ill" (quoted by Cabot, vol. II, p. 734). As mere products of nature, men are not true individuals at all. But the development of the intellectual faculties in man produces an individual in the true sense of the term, one who can transcend the common nature and impose his personality upon it, so that under this inhibitory effect the underlying nature becomes "dormant." "As the reflective faculties open, this subsides" (X, 75). It is because he ceases to share in the immediate possession of the common essence of all things, and develops into a separate entity, that "the individual is always mistaken," and therefore our prime duty is to "surrender" our will, that is, to remove the inhibitory effect of the understanding upon the divinity within us; in other words, to go into a perpetual state of "ecstasy." When we do so, the Soul lives through us, and is genius or is virtue or is love in a man, according as it "breathes through" his intellect or his will or his affection (II, 255). Later, his realization that "all nature is ecstatic" led Emerson to feel that the animal also must yield to nature in order to realize "his highest point;" that the difference in intelligence and even in morality is "only of less and more" (X, 178); but this line of thought came to him too late in life, and he stops short with it before going very far.

But though Emerson considered that "ecstasy" is a state in which the activity of the understanding is partially or totally suspended, and a deeper, instinctive nature asserts itself, yet the difficulty of this for psychology is fundamental. Since this divinity or "reason" is "complete and perfect in every man," is "adult already in the infant man," it follows that the suspension of our ordinary thinking faculties would make deities of us all. Leaving aside all equally obvious objections, this theory leaves a complete dualism in the mind of man. In so far as it has any further interest for us, therefore, Emerson's intuition theory relates itself not to his philosophical but to his religious insights, and as such we must take our final account of it.

CHAPTER VII.

THE RELIGIOUS IMPLICATIONS OF EMERSON'S PHILOSOPHY: THE
NATURE OF GOD; HUMAN RESPONSIBILITY; IMMORTALITY.

The state which Emerson describes as "ecstasy" was in his own case one of religious enthusiasm, superinduced largely, as with all mystics, by the strain of a lofty contemplation, but of course without any of the vulgar features which attended the ecstasies of those mystics whose condition was brought about by abnormal or unhealthy processes. His natural sanity and normal habits of life contributed to make his "subliminal self" well balanced,—with none of the fetid and disordered dreams so common in this condition. Presumably his moments of profound ecstasy were very occasional, for of this he himself complains; and his later attempts at philosophical construction, such as the *Natural History of Intellect,* contain no more of the old fervor than would naturally be due to previous habit. In his admirable essay on Emerson, Mr. John Jay Chapman notes that the mystical mood comes to us all, even in health, but is then only momentary, while with Emerson it was a prevailing habit; and this is true. But Emerson himself tells us that the "mood" varies from the slightest .thrill of virtuous emotion to enthusiasm and ecstasy. Only his occasional and deepest moments, therefore, can justly be considered as being due to an abnormal condition.

What seems actually to have led Emerson to his belief in intuition is the peculiar emotional experience which seems to have attended it; he was "strangely affected" by any unusual experience, by "seeing the shore from a moving ship" and the like. "The least change in our point of view gives the whole world a pictorial air;" that is to say, it introduces a feeling of unreality (I, 55). Even as late as 1844, when this condition must have been passing away, he writes, "Life wears to me a visionary face." Implicitly he argues from his psychological state to the reality of what he believes causes that state. The experience, as Mr. Chapman says, is one common to all. There is a feeling of "otherness" which attends the discovery or reception of such a large and new idea as is related somehow to the soul's growth. Even when one is working over a problem in Mathematics, bewildered and blinded by the mere figures, and suddenly the whole large solution of it comes over him, then he seems to himself to see with other eyes; let the new discovery have a life significance and it is perfectly natural to attribute it to a divine revelation.[88]

There are two ways in which a belief in intuition may be interpreted. It is possible for one to accept his own intuitions, asserting their infallibility without proof; or he may lack confidence in himself and his own intuitions, but recognize their possibility in other and holier men than he, and accept unquestioningly what those claiming to be so inspired have said. In the former class were the great majority of the lesser members of the Transcendental group; in the latter class were those who, puzzled with the multifarious problems of the period we are studying, found peace and rest in the authority of the church of Rome. And not only in the Catholic reaction, but in the development of such conservatism as Goethe's the tendency of the believer in intuitions is often away from the individualism of his own perceptions to the acceptance of what is universal,—the result of the intuition of all men; so that it is not uncommon to find the Transcendentalist a defender of prevailing institutions. Emerson's attitude shows something of a compromise between these two extremes. On the one side was his constant preaching of self-reliance,—the necessary result of the belief that "not I speak but the Father speaketh through me;" on the other side that eager, expectant attitude with which he listened,—"hungrily" it is said,—to the opinions of all about him. His faith in persons, said Bronson Alcott, amounted almost to superstition.[89] The seeming inconsistency of this is resolvable in Emerson's gradual inclining toward the second belief, that any other might have a finer insight, a loftier imagination than his own. It is doubtful if he would have taught his great principle of self-reliance so insistently and incessantly if he had not been by nature self-distrustful. Intuitions, he felt, must be tested by their conformity to the moral law; they are to be got, not by an effort of will, but by self-renunciation; they are to be prepared for by purity in life and thought, and to be worked out in character and action.

---

[88] If it was this experience of exaltation that led Emerson to his belief in himself and his religious reverence for his own intuitions, the reason for his taking seriously the inspirational claims of his associates could easily be found, I think, in his interpreting in the light of his own emotion the difference between their ordinary and their serious conversation. Margaret Fuller and Bronson Alcott, for example, in their published writings have little of philosophical value, for here they wrote in propria persona, so to speak; yet their personal impression on such men as Emerson was very great. An "inspirational lecturer" who seemed to me somewhat left over from Transcendental days, betrayed in a private conversation a difference almost incredible between his attitude of mind when concerned with the petty and annoying affairs of every-day life, and when talking about the deeper things of life.

[89] Life of Emerson, p. 46.

And thus it was, with these Transcendentalists, that no faith or phase of faith, even if it had been "revealed" by a previous "intuition," could stand before a new flood of light. Brownson, one of the most typical of the Transcendentalists, went from creed to creed, each time knowing that at last he was right, and the last time (or two) knowing that he "could not be wrong." It is this assurance in the face of the obvious impossibility of confirmation that makes mysticism essentially a matter of faith, and that makes all faith, to the extent that it is faith merely, a matter of mysticism. Thus faith must always have its psychological explanation, and must be essentially super-rational or it is not *faith* at all. It can never allow for doubt on the one hand, or for proof on the other.

Before considering what were the religious implications of Emerson's philosophy, we must take account of one other element essential to a correct understanding of his attitude. Beyond what I have called his habit of lofty contemplation and his sense of the unreality of things, there was in Emerson a certain childlike simplicity of mind which made him feel himself, as he seemed to others, to belong to the very scheme of things,—a certain sublime naturalness which led Theodore Parker to say that he thanked God in his prayers for the sun, moon, and Emerson. This feeling of kinship to nature and to God seems to be essential to the true mystic, and to be the very foundation of his faith, whether it take the form of the profound philosophic speculations of a Spinoza or the sweet childish babblings of a William Blake. The occult relation which in 1832 Emerson felt in the Jardin des Plantes to exist between the animals and man,[90] and which still appeared occult to him after forty years of philosophizing (X, 20), joined with his sense of the immanence of God and the transitoriness of the "surfaces" amid which we live, was itself, and without any special psychological condition, sufficient basis for a mystical philosophy.

It has been said, upon how complete data of evidence I do not know,[91] that no crime is possible to the "subjective mind" which would not be possible to the subject in his waking state. However this may be, it would seem that one's sub-conscious nature is largely (if not wholly) what he has made it. Emerson's remarkable purity of heart, his elevation of thought, the beauty and serenity of his life, led him to recognize the deity within him as of that large and passive make which we find smiling so blandly through his pages. For as "the poor Indian whose untutored mind" coins a deity after his own pattern, when in a moment

[90] Cabot, vol. II, p. 710.
[91] Thomas Jay Hudson: *Law of Psychic Phenomena.*

of deep mysticism he watches the sun go down into "naked space" and feels the night creep closer about him, so the enlightened Emerson subtends his arc of divinity to cover his own conception of the universe. There is a deep and essential truth in the perverted saying that "man created God in his own image,"—for how could it be other? No revelation, even, could tell us more than we are capable of conceiving. "The god of the cannibals will be a cannibal, of the crusaders a crusader, and of the merchants a merchant," says Emerson himself (VI, 196).

When we come to consider what Emerson has to say as to the first of the three great postulates of religion, concerning the nature and existence of God, we find a most curious combination of intuitive perception with philosophical deduction. Working quietly and with all due philosophical decorum on the necessity of this "unbounded substance" or "illimitable essence," he is wont suddenly to burst into a rhapsody of fervid assurance, apparently conceiving of God as a personal Being; which sudden intuition he immediately tries to bury in the argument upon which it has unwarrantedly intruded. "O my brothers, God exists. There is a soul at the center of nature and over the will of every man, so that none of us can wrong the universe" (II, 132). With the fervor of the prophet always creeps in the symbolism of the poet; almost before he knows it the word is spoken; the secret which cannot be known has been proclaimed abroad.

But how far is it possible to reconcile the God of Emerson's faith with the God of his philosophy? Was he, in the last analysis, theist or pantheist? In making statements which imply now the theistic and now the pantheistic conception, Emerson merely wishes to hold himself aloof, somehow, from committing himself to either point of view. It was again his feeling that the perfect truth lay deeper than any actual expression of it. In the same attitude he even goes so far as to say that he had reason for believing in Unitarianism and the other ism at the same time.[92] And so Emerson nowhere expressly denies either side of this great question. When he speaks of coming upon a secret which "sweeps out of men's minds all vestige of theism" (VI, 302), it is only the beliefs which "their fathers held" that he means. It is this conception of God that he repudiates with so much lofty scorn. "When we have broken our god of tradition and ceased from our god of rhetoric, then may God fire the heart with his presence" (II, 274). Parker felt that Emerson was always a theist, though his vagueness in the use of terms laid him open to the pantheistic charge, and Holbeach claims not only that Emerson

---

[92] Quoted by Dr. M. D. Conway in *The Critic* for May 1903.

is theistic but that all good theism is transcendental.[93] The most definite defense of Emerson's theism seems to me that of Mr. G. W. Cooke:

"To limit Emerson's idea of the Infinite Spirit to what he has said directly about God would be to do him a great injustice. His idea of God is presupposed in his idea of the soul, and must be studied in conjunction with it. The conception he entertains of the soul necessitates belief in God as a supreme intelligent Existence. A thinking soul cannot hold communion with an unthinking essence." [93a]

This seems to me perhaps a trifle arbitrary as an interpretation of Emerson's thought as a whole; for whether it possible or not, Emerson seems to have believed finally that this underlying Reality arrives at consciousness in man, and that this is all the "communion" there is:—it is essentially a soliloquy. That God has any other means of self-communication than this, Emerson does not teach; that which is "Reason" in man, in Nature is only "Spirit,"—an impersonal reality whose eternal progress is fully reflected in its "gigantic shadow."

But this seems to confine God to a very limited and recent selfhood, and to exaggerate the importance of man to an infinite degree. It brings us near to the conclusions of a contemporary critic: "Pantheism sinks man and nature in God; Materialism sinks God and man in the universe; Transcendentalism sinks God and nature in man." [94] Years later Emerson himself wrote in his Journal, "Transcendentalism says, the Man is all" (VII, 268). But Emerson could scarcely stop just here. Man cannot be the culmination of Nature, for man is a failure when viewed in such a light (I, 192). But "to questions of this sort," says Emerson, "Nature replies, 'I grow.' . . . 'I have ventured so great a stake as my success in no single creature, I have not yet arrived at any end'" (pp. 193, 194). That is to say, God may yet attain to a degree of self-realization in some conscious entity more perfect than we—for "Nature can only be conceived as existing to a universal and not to a particular end" (p. 192), although "the termination of the world in a man appears to be the last victory of intelligence" (p. 195). In taking this teleological tone, Emerson does not mean to imply conscious purpose or foresight; all he can find is "one superincumbent tendency"; merely the faith that "there is no chance and no anarchy in the universe. All is system and gradation" (VI, 308). Purpose is not imposed upon a passive universe but is the very constitution of things. "Every star in heaven is discontented and insatiable" (I, 202).

---

[93] *Contemporary Review*, vol. XXIX, p. 481.

[93a] *Ralph Waldo Emerson: His Life, Writings, and Philosophy*, p. 288.

[94] *American Whig Review*, vol. I, p. 233. Not signed, but written by William B. Greene.

But when we speak of the "evolution of God," of his "arriving" at consciousness only in man, we are talking in terms of the phenomenal world. Surely Emerson knew that God and the world of reality transcend space and time, for he has said so clearly and repeatedly. Then if this self-realization is not a temporal process, why may not any of the great tenets of theism be true? Consciousness in the part may not imply consciousness in the totality, but if we rise above these phenomenal limitations, does it in the least preclude self-consciousness in the totality?

When he came to considerations of this sort, Emerson seems to have been unable to think consistently or even clearly. It would require more than special pleading to find in whatever growth there may be in his system any increasingly profound comprehension of this problem. He always gives, or means to give, a complete adherence to Kant's doctrine: at the very start he assumes this point of view; later he writes, "Time and space are but physiological colors which the eye makes, but the soul is light" (II, 66), which is a fairly adequate translation into his own poetic language of the main conception of the Transcendental Aesthetic; and after he had come into his period of more prosaic phraseology he says punctiliously (if somewhat arbitrarily) that "science has come to treat space and time as simply forms of thought" (VI, 303). But in spite of all this, I believe that Emerson never did and never could free himself from a practical belief in the Lockean conception. As Kant himself says, we cannot think space away from objects, or time out of events; and however often Emerson may have disposed of these elements philosophically, he still found himself compelled to reckon with them. In spite of his transcendental tone he can say, "My eyes and ears are revolted by any neglect of the physical facts" (I, 189); and however he might reason himself away from these, to these he always returned. An interesting instance of this occurs in the most profoundly mystical of all his essays, where, after showing how the "Over-Soul" is above all our limitations, such as space and time, he proceeds with an elaboration of this idea from a wholly poetic standpoint, and returns to note the soul's advances by a metamorphosis in which time is an essential element (II, 256-258). And later, again, in his recognition of "boundless space and boundless time" as "the two cardinal conditions" of nature (III, 173), he shows clearly that his conception was at best really Spinoza's and not Kant's.

If there is no room in Emerson's philosophy for a theistic conception of God by a removal of the ultimately impersonal element with the removal of the limitations of time and space, is there any other means by which this mere background of being may be raised to become the actual

God of Emerson's apparently unhesitating faith? Such arguments as that there must be a God to satisfy the cravings of the universe are not arguments at all, and to this level Emerson seldom descends. The nearest approach to a reconciliation lies in the references he makes to God as "the Soul of the world," the suggestion for which he may have got, like the Stoics themselves, from Plato. But this conception is not quite true to his main theory; for in reducing the relation between mind and matter to an actual substance underlying both, the body-soul simile of which the Stoics make so much is no longer possible. If God were only one of the results of the evolution of this primordial substance, or one aspect of it, there would be something in the universe "older and deeper" and more inclusive than God himself; and in such a conception Emerson could never believe. In remaining a mystic and adhering to his belief in immanence as against transcendence to the very end, Emerson was forced to remain, as he always was, a pantheist. "When I speak of God," said Emerson once, "I prefer to say It—It." [95]

On the freedom of the individual Emerson's whole philosophy was based, and all refractory elements were forced to accord first of all with this apparent fact. Yet it must be admitted that the possibility of individual freedom is ultimately unanalyzable, that even with Emerson it is a clear perception of the intuition and no more. And again, though he has said so much of high interest concerning immortality, yet Emerson is careful not to draw too positive a conclusion as to this mighty mystery. Indeed, this is his one subject of grave doubt. The reason for this is as interesting as it is apparent. During his moments of intuition he might readily "perceive" the existence of God or his own freedom, but he could scarcely *foresee* the fact of his immortality. On this account he was compelled to take the subject out of the sphere of argument altogether. "Future state is an illusion for the ever-present state. It is not length of life but depth of life. It is not duration, but a talking of the soul out of time, as all high action of the mind does" (VIII, 329). But in arguing that we cannot argue about this subject, because in our moments of intuition we perceive that we are in our highest state immortal, we come upon the most delightful of paradoxes; we may be immortal for a time, and then, as we descend from this state of exaltation, we may cease to be immortal! If we are really serious in our abolishing of time, the very word Immortality has no meaning. As much as this Emerson practically admits when he says, "These questions which we lust to ask about the future are a confession of sin. God has no answer for them. No answer

---

[95] Recorded by D. G. Haskins in *Ralph Waldo Emerson: His Maternal Ancestors*, p. 130.

in words can reply to a question of things" (II, 266). He means that
that which is personal to each one is not the "soul," which is "perfect
and identical in all," but those later developed faculties of the understanding, and that therefore immortality is a question of the "understanding" and cannot be answered by the "reason."

In spite of himself, however, Emerson can not quite get away from
the question of a personal immortality. But beginning with doubt on
this subject,[96] he ends in utter negation, though he is said to have looked
forward at the time of his death with some hope of a future recognition.
Even in the essay in which he most constantly asserts his belief, he is
constrained to admit that he sees no place for it in his system: "I confess that everything connected with our personality fails. Nature never
spares the individual" (VIII, 325). Sometimes his faith rises to the
point of saying, "If it is best that conscious personal life shall continue,
it will continue" (VIII, 313); and he offers by way of justification of
this faith that "The ground of hope is in the infinity of the world; which
infinity reappears in every particle, the powers of all society in every individual, and of all mind in every mind" (p. 316); or, more definitely,
"If we follow it out, this demand in our thought for an ever-onward action is the argument for immortality" (VI, 279). But even this he feels
at last is futile. "An individual body is the momentary arrest or fixation
of certain atoms, which, after performing compulsory duty to this en-
chanted statue, are released again to flow in the currents of the world.
An individual mind in like manner is a fixation or momentary eddy in
which certain services and powers are taken up and minister in petty
niches and localities, and then, being released, return to the unbounded
soul of the world" (XII, 25).

This is his last word, in his final excursion in philosophy, *The
Natural History of Intellect.* There is something strangely sad about
this last philosophical attempt of a man who had built his whole life's
argument on the belief that he could *know,* as he clings bravely to the
memory of his better insights, and struggles forward with the broken
remnants of a philosophy which had once been so full of bright promise
and eager hope.

We find, then, that Emerson's doctrine of intuition is futile also in
the purer realm of religion. The best that Emerson can say is the best
that we all say, and no more. To prove the existence of a personal God
would rob us of our right of faith, which needs only that philosophy shall

---

[96] At twenty-three he writes in his Journal (II, 178): "I believe myself immortal. The beam of the balance trembles, to be sure, but settles always on the
right side. For otherwise all things look so silly. The sun is silly . . ."

not preclude the possibility,—as surely it does not; to prove human freedom and responsibility is to prove what in the heart of us we all know, however hardened determinists we may clam to be; to prove immortality would be only, at best, the deifying of Paley, the putting of a prudential motive on all our conduct. In applying his "philosophy of intuition" to the great postulates of religion, Emerson was only proving again the final negative answer to the Transcendental Dialectic.

We have tested Emerson by the highest standards. May we not conclude that he failed to do, in the great guesses of philosophy and religion, only what the greatest philosophers themselves have failed to do, namely, to give a definite answer to our fundamental problems? Before he meets his final failure he comes, it seems to me, very far along the road of a consistent idealism; and in the account that he does take of the nature and workings of intuition he comes as close as anyone has yet come to the making of Mysticism a philosophy; and he makes the one definite contribution of showing why, if Mysticism be true, it cannot be explained in philosophical terms. The acceptance of Emerson's philosophy is, like that philosophy itself, a piece of pure mysticism. It may be recognition but it is never conviction. However sober and well ordered his argument may be for a time, it is always the religious instinct that is speaking, and only he who hath ears to hear can receive the message. In Emerson's own poetic language, "Jove nods to Jove from behind each of us."

It is in this very fact that his greatness lies. If he had made a more philosophical appeal, I doubt if his importance would be half so great. For as it is the religious instinct that receives such truths, so religious men are always the discoverers and prophets,—never philosophers, or those whose appeal is to the intellect primarily. It is on account of its religious nature that the appeal of mysticism, either at first or second hand, is so overpowering when it comes.

CHAPTER VIII.

EMERSON'S ETHICS: THE MORAL LAW;   ORIGIN OF THE VIRTUES;
OPTIMISM.

I have attempted to show that Emerson in his own peculiar and original way worked through the central problem of metaphysics till he came
to the Dark Tower itself. At least I am not aware that any thinker has
actually gone farther with pure philosophic theory than did Emerson in
his deepest insights; though of course when the masters have broken
the way the mere learner may easily come as far. Emerson's philosophy
is negative not only in that it goes sufficiently far and with sufficient consistency to show that a rational explanation of the universe is impossible
along Transcendental lines, but more positively negative, so to speak, in
that it leads inevitably to the conclusion that the final and highest result
of such philosophizing is the giving up of philosophy for questions of
more practical value. And so Transcendentalism, as I said at the beginning of this essay, means little or nothing apart from its practical application.

Emerson's thinking along the lines of ethics is not to be taken as
the mere talk of a cultured gentleman. It is a consistent part of his
idealism. Blandly superficial as he is so often and as he seems so habit-
ually, he still has sufficient depth to make us return again and again with
increased respect for the calm majesty of his thought and the high consistency of his purpose:—the purpose of bringing to the average thinking man a vital concern with these subjects,—of these subjects so sterile
and unprofitable in the hands of our technical theorists. But here Emerson's work commands our greater respect, since in his thinking along these
lines he was more of an anticipator of later writers than in his philosophy
he was an unconscious follower of the thinkers before him.

But the same things which have led men to pass by Emerson's philosophy so lightly have prevented their giving to his ethics the attention
it deserves. Since Emerson's day we have mortgaged to our scholars the
entire estate of learning; we have become trespassers if we dare to think
outside the schools. Emerson dared; and the makers of our scholastic
caste have snubbed him roundly for it. On the other hand, to those who
would gladly accept him as a writer on ethics, even while denying him
the rank of a philosopher, his manner of stating his principles offers the

same obstacles. His method is still statement and restatement of his central point of view, always the same though seen in many different aspects, never bolstered up by deduction or burdened by logical proof—impertinent to one who sees the fact as fact.[97] We should now have, in consequence, an equal task in educing his theory from his poetic form were it not that his ethical teachings are an obvious corollary of his idealism. There is no more in Emerson's ethics than the translation and elaboration of his philosophical dicta in ethical terms; indeed the ethics implies the philosophy just as much as the philosophy entails the ethics.

The coming to the plane of consciousness, it will be remembered, is regarded by Emerson as the "fall of man" (III, 77). Spirit no longer works according to its own perfect laws. "And the blindness of the intellect begins when it would be something of itself. The weakness of the will begins when the individual would be something of himself" (II, 255). This doctrine of the "lapse," which Bronson Alcott had absorbed probably from his reading of Plotinus and had poured forth in his solemn manner into Emerson's credulous ears, was applied by the latter unflinchingly to his newly formulated theory of evolution, and thus formed the basis of his ethics. We have the attainment of a moral will at the expense of innocence. And the law applies not only to us but to all creation. "The men, though young, having tasted the first drop from the cup of thought, are already dissipated; the maples and ferns are still uncorrupt; yet no doubt when they come to consciousness they too will curse and swear" (III, 174).

But back of individual freedom are the fast laws of fate, as we call all operation of law in the outer world (VI, 211). Of these laws, as I have already noted, the highest and all-inclusive is the moral law. The moral law, which in us is the moral sentiment (*Ib.*), is the very groundwork of our being, and thus not only we but in a deep sense total nature is moral. "For though the new element of freedom and an individual has been admitted, yet the primordial atoms are prefigured and predestined to moral issues, are in search of justice, and ultimate right is done" (VI, 209).

In remembering these two complementary principles, the whole ethics of Emerson becomes apparent at a glance. Since the universe is essentially moral, "Virtue is the adherence in action to the nature of things" (II, 151); which is only another way of saying that a man possesses all virtues when he is possessed by the great Source of all. "If he have found his centre, the Deity will shine through him" (II, 269). By this we are raised "not into a particular virtue, but into the region of

<hr />

[97] Compare W. T. Harris in the *Atlantic Monthly,* vol. L, pp. 238 ff.

all the virtues . . . so there is a kind of descent and accommodation felt when we leave speaking of moral nature to urge a virtue which it enjoins. . . . The heart which abandons itself to the Supreme Mind finds itself related to all its works, and will travel a royal road to particular knowledges and powers" (II, 258).

The means to the attainment of this great end, this *summum bonum,* so far as it requires volitional and hence moral action on our part, is obedience. "We need only obey" (II, 132). Obedience is, therefore, in a sense, the only virtue, and even it is not so much a virtue as an "act of piety." While an uncompromising self-surrender is the one condition to this Emersonian "self-realization," yet there is no scourging of the flesh, or triumphant rising of the spirit from victory to victory. It is here that Emerson's Unitarianism asserts itself in opposition to the earlier Congregationalism. "To the well-born child all the virtues are natural and not painfully acquired" (II, 259). Like the later teachers of the "gospel of relaxation," Emerson would have us yield ourselves naturally and with perfect trust and rest, to the great power within us which sustains us and which "constitutes us men."

"In like manner our moral nature is vitiated by any interference of our will. People represent virtue as a struggle, and take to themselves great airs upon their attainments, and the question is everywhere vexed when a noble nature is commended, whether the man is not better who strives with temptation. But there is no merit in the matter. Either God is there or he is not there. . . .

"Not less conspicuous is the preponderance of nature over will in all practical life. . . . That which externally seemed will and immovableness was willingness and self-annihilation. . . .

"The lesson is forcibly taught by these observations that our life might be much easier and simpler than we make it; that the world might be a happier place than it is; that there is no need of struggles, convulsions, and despairs, of the wringing of the hands and the gnashing of the teeth; that we miscreate our own evils. We interfere with the optimism of nature" (II, 127-129).

But this is only one aspect of the matter. Emerson's main contention in his first little book, *Nature,* is that Discipline—the moral education of man—may be "The Final Cause of the Universe." On this seemingly contradictory point of view he insists again, thirty years later, in a second essay on "Character": "On the perpetual conflict between the dictate of this universal mind and the wishes and interests of the individual, the moral discipline of life is built. The one craves a private benefit, which the other requires him to renounce out of respect to the absolute good" (X, 96). And with a psychological insight as remarkable in

Emerson as it is rare, he tells how this morality dependent upon freedom is produced. "But insight is not will, nor is affection will. . . . There must be a fusion of these two to generate the energy of will" (VI, 33). I might well have paused over the metaphysical and psychological significance of this sentence; but I have chosen to give it only its ethical bearing, since it is not an integral part of Emerson's Transcendentalism.

Of the origin of conscience, Emerson has therefore this account to offer: "I see the unity of thought and of morals running through all animated nature; there is no difference of quality, but only of more and less. . . . The man down in nature occupies himself in guarding, in feeding, in warming and multiplying his body, and, as long as he knows no more, we justify him; but presently a mystic change is wrought, a new perception opens, and he is made a citizen of the world of souls; he feels what is called duty; he is aware that he owes a higher allegiance to do and live as a good member of this universe. In the measure in which he has this sense he is a man, rises to the universal life. The high intellect is absolutely at one with moral nature" (X, 178).

From this account of the origin of the virtues, their classification becomes an easy matter. "There is no virtue which is final" (II, 295). "The same law of eternal procession ranges all that we call the virtues, and extinguishes each in the light of a better" (II, 293). There is, then, a hierarchy in the virtues, the lower and simpler, of course, being the earliest produced. We pass from the individual virtue of physical courage, which is the mere "affection" of love joined with the "insight"of its universal value in opposition to and triumph over the self-conserving instinct of fear; to the personal virtues of chastity and temperance, by which we improve our own natures and make them more effective to universal ends at the expense of and triumph over our natural appetites and inclinations; to the third and final type of virtue, exemplified in justice and love, which are the public virtues, and show the active operation of virtue where it exists at its fullest—in our relation to others. The public virtue, justice, will of course have its own stages of development in the history of civilization. "The civil history of men might be traced by the successive ameliorations as marked in higher moral generalizations;—virtue meaning physical courage, then chastity and temperance, then justice and love;—bargains of kings with peoples of certain rights to certain classes, then of rights to masses,—then at last came the day when, as historians rightly tell, the nerves of the world were electrified by the proclamation that all men are born free and equal" (X, 181).

But if the one condition to the attainment of virtue is personal freedom, its prime essential is a certain austerity of manner. To the highest

success ease and comfort are fatal. "He who aims high must dread an
easy home and popular manners" (VI, 155). As with Hegel, there is no
virtue but in the overcoming of vice. "Nature is upheld by antagonism.
. . . without enemies, no hero. . . . the glory of character is in affront-
ing the horrors of depravity to draw thence new nobilities of power" (VI,
242). "Let us replace sentimentalism by realism;" cries our idealist and
"dreamer" (VI, 206). "Nature, as we know her, is no saint. . . . Her
darlings, the great, the strong, the beautiful, are not children of our law;
do not come out of the Sunday School, nor weigh their food, nor punctu-
ally keep the commandments" (III, 66). From this "realism" the ethical
deduction is inevitable:

"We wish to learn philosophy by rote, and play at heroism. But the
wiser God says, Take the shame, the poverty and the penal solitude that
belong to truth-speaking. Try the rough water as well as the smooth.
Rough water can teach lessons worth knowing. When the state is un-
quiet, personal qualities are more than ever decisive. Fear not a revolution which will constrain you to live five years in one. Don't be so tender
at making an enemy now and then. Be willing to go to Coventry sometimes, and let the populace bestow on you their coldest contempts. The
finished man of the world must eat of every apple once. He must hold
his hatreds also at arm's length, and not remember spite. He has neither
friends nor enemies, but values men only as channels of power" (VI,
155).

We are now ready to confront the problem of Emerson's reconciliation, if he has one, of his two main ethical doctrines,—the absence of all
struggle in the attainment of all virtue in self-surrender, and the "perpetual conflict" of the will, upon which the very essence of morality is
based, and by which the separate virtues were produced. Emerson's own
answer, if he were brought face to face with it, might be one of those
maddening, frank admissions of both sides of a flat contradiction. "This
is true, and that other is true. But our geometry cannot span these extreme points and reconcile them" (VI, 10). There is, however, in this
case, as so often, only a seeming contradiction. The inconsistency is the
same as in the case of universal spirit and individual selfhood and freedom, and is capable of a corresponding resolution. "From this transfer
of the world into the consciousness, this beholding of all things in the
mind, follow easily his [the idealist's] whole ethics. It is simpler to be
self-dependent. The height, the deity of man is to be self-sustained, to
need no gift, no foreign force" (I, 315). And from his idealism, consistently also, comes his practical ethics: "Do not cumber yourself with
fruitless pains to mend and remedy remote effects; let the soul be erect,
and all things will go well" (Ib.). On the other hand, from the equally

primary fact of human freedom comes of necessity the need of sin and struggle. "In morals, wild liberty breeds iron conscience" (VI, 65).

But as each virtue is extinguished "in the light of a better," the final virtue will be, obviously, as with Spencer, the rising to a supra-virtuous plane; virtue will be "its own reward" because it is no longer difficult but natural and inevitable. Each intermediate good involves its struggle of will, but the "highest good" is when the will negates itself, which is the last step in our "self-realization." The individual must "lose his life" in the great Reality in order "to find it." This, on the one hand, is no more than an ethical rendering of the religion of Jesus, of the philsophy of Hegel, of the poetic insight of Goethe. But on the other hand, Emerson is as thorough-going and up-to-date a Eudæmonist as any among us;[98] though we might perhaps coin for his ethics the name of Eleutherianism, since the self-realization culminates in perfect freedom, supravolitional, as the final and highest good. And in this I find no contradiction, but an ethical insight wise and far-reaching.

"And so I think that the last lesson of life, the choral song which rises from all elements and all angels, is a voluntary obedience, a necessitated freedom. Man is made of the same atoms as the world is, he shares the same impressions, predispositions, and destiny. When his mind is illuminated, when his heart is kind, he throws himself joyfully into the sublime order, and does, with knowledge, what the stones do by structure" (VI, 229).

It will be seen from all this how it is that Emerson's ethics culminates in so absolute an optimism. Professor Santayana says that Emerson had no sufficient warrant for his optimism, that it was only "a pious tradition" from the religion of his ancestors, that survived in him as an instinct; and suggests that he allowed "his will and his conscience to be hypnotized by the spectacle of a necessary evolution." [99] Mr. Inge, also, though writing in a wholly different strain, tells us that there is no comfort in Emerson's optimism, because it is blind;[100] and many others, after reading the flat absurdities in the over-famous essay on "Compensation," have felt that Emerson's optimism could be nothing but a wilful disregarding of the facts of life. Even his fellow Transcendentalists, especially Margaret Fuller, felt a certain "aloofness" about him, and accused him of never coming close to reality. To a certain extent there was a

---

[98] Hedge regards Emerson simply as a Stoic because of the "emphasis with which he affirms right to be the absolute good, right for its own sake, not for any foreign benefit." (*Literary World*, XI, 176.)

[99] *Poetry and Religion*, pp. 228, 229.

[100] *Christian Mysticism*, p. 321.

temperamental serenity about Emerson which went far to make the optimism of his daily life; he preferred always to put the bright side forward; yet no one was ever more deeply concerned with "things as they are," or faced more unflinchingly or with keener sympathy the tragedy and imperfections of life. But these things were to him partial, and he kept his eyes fastened on the totality, which he still judged to be good. That which distinguishes Emerson from his fellow Transcendentalists is not absence of the emotional but presence of the intellectual.

It is worth noting that Emerson contends always that "Nature is reckless of the individual" (VI, 133), and that if "the final cause of the world is to make holy or wise or beautiful men, we see that it has not succeeded" (I, 192). In justice to this neglected side of Emerson's view of things, I may be pardoned for quoting his splendid and stirring condemnation of the aspirations and pleasures of men:

"Read alternately in natural and in civil history, a treatise of astronomy, for example, with a volume of French *Mémoires pour servir.* When we have spent our wonder in computing this wasteful hospitality with which boon nature turns off new firmaments without end into her wide common, as fast as the madrepores make coral,—suns and planets hospitable to souls,—and then shorten the sight to look into this court of Louis Quatorze, and see the game that is played there,—duke and marshal, abbé and madame,—a gambling table where each is laying traps for the other, where the end is ever by some lie or fetch to outwit your rival and ruin him with this solemn fop in wig and stars,—the king;—one can hardly help asking if this planet is a fair specimen of the so generous astronomy, and if so, whether the experiment have not failed, and whether it be quite worth while to make more, and glut the innocent space with so poor an article" (I, 192).

And the mass of men fares no better at his hands:

"In our large cities the population is godless, materialized,—no bond, no fellow-feeling, no enthusiasm. These are not men, but hungers, thirsts, fevers and appetites walking. How is it people manage to live on,—so aimless as they are? After their pepper-corn aims are gained, it seems as if the lime in their bones alone held them together, and not any worthy purpose. There is no faith in the intellectual, none in the moral universe. . . . In creeds never was such levity; witness the heathenisms of Christianity, the periodic 'revivals,' the Millennium mathematics, the peacock ritualism, the retrogression to Popery, the maundering of Mormons, the squalor of Mesmerism, the deliration of rappings, the rat and mouse revelation, thumps in table-drawers, and black art. The architecture, the music, the prayer, partake of the madness; the arts sink into shift and make-believe. Not knowing what to do, we ape our ancestors; the churches stagger backward to the mummeries of the Dark Ages" (VI, 199, 200).

But back of all this, which is surely a sufficient account of the dark side of life, the optimism of Emerson is unshaken. "In front of these sinister facts, the first lesson of history is the good of evil" (VI, 240). It is the method of nature to play off vice against vice. "Most of the great results of history are brought about by discreditable means" (VI, 243). To Emerson in his more poetic mood, the purple mountain and the ancient wood declare

> "That Night or Day, that Love or Crime,
> Leads all souls to the Good" (IX, 78).

Emerson had as much faith as Horace Bushnell in the "moral uses of dark things." "In our life and culture everything is worked up and comes in use,—passion, war, revolt, bankruptcy, and not less, folly and blunders, insult, ennui and bad company" (VI, 249). This attitude of Emerson is well illustrated by an incident recorded by Edward Everett Hale.[101] They were considering a college youth who had taken many honors and established a brilliant record. "I did not know he was so fine a fellow," said Emerson. "And now, if something will fall out amiss,— if he should be unpopular with his class, or if his father should fail in business, or if some other misfortune can befall him,—all will be well." This was not cynicism or paradox but sincere conviction.

The first and most obvious argument for Emerson's optimism is that it is the ethical reading of the great fact of evolution. David Lee Maulsby, in a doctoral dissertation on *The Contribution of Emerson to Literature* (1911), makes Emerson's "unqualified optimism" a corollary of the doctrine of the immanence of God; Professor James finds it one of the philosophical directions of his states of mystical ecstasy;[102] Augustine Birrell considers that it "rests on his theory of *compensation*";[103] W. Robertson Nicoll calls it a "direct inference" from certain of Emerson's "propositions" which seem to me rather to be derived from his optimism than to have given rise to it;[104] William F. Dana believes Emerson's optimism purely intellectual and not at all derived from Christian dogma;[105] Francis Grierson states that "the explanation of Emerson's optimism lies in his intellectual aloofness, his mental indifference to things beneath the plane on which he lived."[106] For all these divergent views, and others, warrant can be found in the essays. But only in his

---

[101] *Works*, vol. VIII, p. 256.
[102] *Varieties of Religious Experience*, p. 416.
[103] *Emerson: a Lecture*, p. 41.
[104] *North American Review*, CLXXVI, 678.
[105] *The Optimism of Ralph Waldo Emerson*, p. 53.
[106] *The Celtic Temperament*, p. 93.

evolution doctrine can I find an ethical basis for this famous optimism which everyone feels he must explain. As such, at least, it needs neither explanation nor apology. "We only insist that the man meliorate, and that the plant grow upward and convert the base into the better nature" (VI, 246) ; "Meliorism is the law. The cruelest foe is a masked benefactor" (X, 182). Yet in the last analysis this argument for optimism also resolves itself into a mere statement of larger faith:

"If the Divine Providence has hid from men neither disease nor deformity nor corrupt society, but has stated itself out in passions, in war, in trade, in the love of power and pleasure, in hunger and need, in tyrannies, literatures and arts,—let us not be so nice that we cannot write these facts down coarsely as they stand, or doubt but there is a counterstatement as ponderous, which we can arrive at, and which, being put, will make all square. The solar system has no anxiety about its reputation, and the credit of truth and honesty is as safe; nor have I any fear that a skeptical bias can be given by leaning hard on the sides of fate, of practical power, or of trade, which the doctrine of Faith cannot downweigh" (VI, 194).

From this it would appear that optimism is only another name for faith. If so, Professor Santayana is quite right in saying that there is no philosophical basis for the optimism of Emerson, but that it was due to his religious instinct. One sometimes wonders if optimism is not always either temperamental or religious in its origin. But this does not in the least imply that it is illogical, or unwarranted, or "blind." Indeed the ultimate warrant of optimism is well put by Emerson in one crisp, ringing sentence: "We grant that human life is mean, but how did we find out that it was mean?" (II, 251). If human nature is wilful and weak, still it is human nature that sees this and condemns it; and however good humanity might grow, the pain of imperfection and the haunting ideal of an ever unrealized good must still be in us to keep the old world going. "Thus journeys the mighty Ideal before us; it never was known to fall into the rear. No man ever came to an experience which was satiating, but his good is tidings of a better. Onward and onward!" (III, 76). Or again:

"The fiend that man harries,
Is love of the best" (IX, 11) ;

and in the pain of this is our perpetual salvation.

It will be seen from this that there is considerable point in making the distinction that there are three stages in Emerson's optimism, corresponding to the three stages in the development of the individual: there is the optimism of the senses, the pessimism of the understanding, and the optimism of the reason.[107]   The first stage is illustrated by Emerson's untiring insistence upon the beauty of nature; the second is seen in the conflict of will with things as they are,—a conflict foredoomed to failure; the third is found when we consider this immediate need of action in its relation to the great scheme of things.   Optimism is still a matter of faith, but it is a faith founded upon reason.   In his essay on "The Sovereignty of Ethics" Emerson writes:

"Thus a sublime confidence is fed at the bottom of the heart that, in spite of appearances, in spite of malignity and blind self-interest living for the moment, an eternal, beneficent necessity is always bringing things right; and, though we should fold our arms,—which we cannot do, for our duty requires us to be the very hands of this guiding sentiment, and work in the present moment,—the evils we suffer will at last end themselves through the incessant opposition of Nature to everything hurtful" (X, 182).

---

[107] J. F. Dutton, in the *Unitarian Review,* vol. XXXV, p. 132.

CHAPTER IX.

EMERSON'S CONTRIBUTION TO SOCIOLOGY: THE INDIVIDUAL AND THE STATE; THE BROOK FARM IDEA; THEORY OF EDUCATION.

No one can have a fundamental philosophy dominating his entire thought, and write upon the subjects of art and society, without implying more or less of an Esthetics and a Sociology. But these, with Emerson, are mere corollaries which might be deduced from his philosophy if he had written no word on either subject. He himself, though from the first he showed a genuine interest in these matters, seems to have become conscious of how his ideas had formulated regarding them after his prime creative impulse had somewhat spent itself in the working out of his idealism; and hence we find separate essays devoted rather to the actual results of his thinking than to a tentative working out of his ideas as they came to him, which is his usual method in treating of philosophic problems. His late and somewhat commonplace essay on Civilization (VII, 23-37), for example, deals directly with the subject matter of Sociology with a definiteness of system and order which shows that Emerson was merely recalling and restating opinions which had long been familiar to him; and much the same thing will be found true of his various essays on art and beauty. Yet as one gives his attention to what Emerson does actually say in the province of Sociology,[108] he becomes again surprised at the rigid *consistency* of his thinking, and at the depth of it.

There are two principles at the basis of Emerson's democracy: (1) the Universal Mind is open to all men, hence all men have a divine right to their opinions; and (2) the great (that is, "representative") man is he who is most open to receive truth, while the many—the mob—are "blind mouths"; so that property, culture, even aristocracy of a sort are essential to any true democracy. In several articles which have appeared in various periodicals, it has been said that Emerson was like Carlyle in his attitude toward the man of genius. I do not see how anyone who had read enough of Emerson to venture a printed opinion could hold such a view. Julian Hawthorne has the right of it in this instance: "He was no hero-worshipper, like Carlyle. A hero was, to him, not so much a power-

---

[108] I use the word in its broadest sense.

ful and dominating personality, as a relatively impersonal instrument of God for the accomplishment of some great end." [109]

It cannot be denied that there was in Emerson, as there was in Shakespeare, an instinctive abhorrence of the "vulgar herd," and a corresponding predilection in favor of good birth and breeding. "For a philosopher," said Walt Whitman the super-democrat, "Emerson possesses a singularly dandified theory of manners." [110] And indeed there is much in Emerson's published utterances which might justify this criticism. "The best are accused of exclusiveness. It would be more true to say they separate as oil and water . . . each seeking his like" (VII, 19). From his very boyhood, we find this attitude of Emerson recorded in his Journals. At nineteen he writes: "From the want of an upper class in society, from the admirable republican equality which levels one with all, results a rudeness and sometimes a savageness of manners which is apt to disgust a polished and courtly man" (J. I, 147).

Much more which might be quoted in this connection seems to stand in contrast to those more typically American sentiments which we may also find abundantly on Emerson's pages, and again the old charge of inconsistency confronts us; and again it is to be answered by noting both sides of the contradiction with their synthesis occurring together in the same essay. Let me cite a passage of each sort from "Considerations by the Way" in the *Conduct of Life* volume:

"Leave this hypocritical prating about the masses. Masses are rude, lame, unmade, pernicious in their demands and influence, and need not to be flattered but to be schooled. . . . The worst of charity is that the lives you are asked to preserve are not worth preserving. Masses! the calamity is the masses. . . . If government knew how, I should like to see it check, not multiply the population. . . . Away with this hurrah of masses, and let us have the considerate vote of single men spoken on their honor and their conscience. In old Egypt it was established law that the vote of a prophet be reckoned equal to a hundred hands. I think it was much under-estimated" (VI, 237).

Is this not rare snobbishness? But look ten pages farther:

"By humiliations, by defects, by loss of sympathy, by gulfs of disparity, learn a wider truth and humanity than that of a fine gentleman. A Fifth-Avenue landlord, a West-End householder, is not the highest style of man; and though good hearts and sound minds are of no condition, yet he who is to be wise for many must not be protected. He must know the huts where poor men lie, and the chores which poor men

---

[109] "Emerson as an American" in *The Genius and Character of Emerson*, p. 68.

[110] *Literary World*, XI, 177.

do. . . . Take him out of his protections. . . . Plant him down among farmers, firemen, Indians, and emigrants. Set a dog on him; set a highwayman on him; try him with a course of mobs; send him to Kansas, to Pike's Peak, to Oregon; and, if he have true faculty, this may be the element he wants, and he will come out of it with broader wisdom and manly power" (VI, 247, 248).

It is the turn of the poor man to point his finger at the pampered rich, and to claim Emerson as his very own! But Emerson's desire regarding rich and poor alike is "to draw individuals out of them":

"The mass are animal, in pupilage, and near chimpanzee. But the units whereof this mass is composed, are neuters, every one of which may be grown to a queen-bee. . . . To say then, the majority are wicked, means no malice, no bad heart in the observer, but simply that the majority are unripe, and have not yet come to themselves, do not know their opinion" (VI, 239, 240).

This, then, is all a part of Emerson's extreme individualism. His attitude toward the State is to be wholly explained by his belief in the ultimate value of each member of the commonwealth either in actuality or in potentiality. And as freedom is the last reach of his eudæmonism, if I read Emerson's Ethics aright, so freedom for the individual should be the final purpose of the State; and to apply this axiom is the purpose of all Sociology. This attitude Emerson takes in his Journal as early as 1827: "Wise men perceive that the advantage of the whole is best consulted in consulting the real advantage of the particular" (J. II, 174); and he is still saying the same thing in his Second Series of Essays in 1844: "The only interest for the consideration of the State is persons . . . the highest end of government is the culture of men" (III, 195). But whether this should result in a democratic or monarchial form of government, in socialism or in anarchy, he is not so sure. With one who persists in seeing both sides of every question it is inevitable that there should be statements looking in each direction.

"Every human society" writes Emerson in his Journal, "wants to be officered by a best class . . . who are adorned with dignity and accomplishments" (J. VIII, 99); yet the fact remains that "thousands of human beings may exercise toward each other the grandest and simplest sentiments as well as a knot of friends, or a pair of lovers" (J. III, 221). In his *English Traits* Emerson has much to say regarding the artificiality, inequality, and even tyrannical nature of the English social system: "The feudal character of the English state, now that it is getting obsolete, glares a little, in contrast with the democratic tendencies. The inequality of power and property shocks republican nerves" (V, 166). But before

he is done, the other side of the matter claims his attention: "The American system is more democratic, more humane; yet the American people
do not yield better or more able men, or more inventions or books or
benefits than the English. Congress is not wiser or better than Parlia-
ment. France has abolished its suffocating old *régime,* but is not recently marked by any more wisdom or virtue" (V, 290). In one mood he
can say, "I am thankful that I am an American as I am thankful that I
am a man" (J. III, 189); and in another mood, "Any form of government would content me in which the rulers were gentlemen" (J. VI, 446).
And all of this means merely that the individual is of prime importance,
and

> "The state may follow how it can,
>   As Olympus follows Jove" (IX, 74).

At times this attitude leads Emerson to the position made famous
by Rousseau: "As if the Union had any other real basis than the good
pleasure of a majority of the citizens to be united" (I, 368); and this
leads on into occasional statements of frank and open anarchy: "Hence
the less government we have the better. . . . To educate the wise man
the State exists, and with the appearance of the wise man the State ex-
pires" (III, 206). Asked by his English friends if any American had an
idea of the right future of this country, he thought not of the statesmen
who would make America another Europe, but "of the simplest and
purest minds; I said, 'Certainly yes;—but those who hold it are fanatics
of a dream which I should hardly care to relate to your English ears, to
which it might be only ridiculous,—and yet it is the only true.' So I
opened the dogma of no-government and non-resistance" (V, 272).

Consistent individualism is bound to end in anarchy. But all the connotation of that word is foreign to Emerson's nature; and his principle
of "non-resistance" renders his principle of "no-government" quite innocent and harmless. At times a threat lurks in the shadow: the principle of church and state is wrong, he says boldly in his Journal, and
vitiates charity and religion; but "I persist in inaction . . . until my hour
comes" (J. V, 294). And after he has refused to join in Ripley's Brook
Farm experiment he seems to excuse his own conscience by saying, "I
do not wish to remove from my present prison to a prison a little larger.
I wish to break all prisons" (J. V, 473).

The same attitude shows in what he has to say regarding the private ownership of land. His whole sympathy, says Salter, was with the
rising tide of social democracy.[111] "Whilst another man has no land,

---

[111] *International Journal of Ethics,* XIII, 414.

my title to mine, your title to yours, is at once vitiated" (I, 224). He even goes so far as to say, or to sing, rather,

"None shall rule but the humble,
And none but Toil shall have" (IX, 175).

Yet on the other hand, when Thoreau inveighed against private property Emerson wrote in his Journal, "I defended, of course, the good institution as a scheme" (J. V, 128); and while protesting that the philosophic class need no possessions he points out that others do, because property is their certificate of merit. "It is very cruel of you to insist, because you can very well forego them, that he shall" (J. IV, 244). The heart of his address on "Man the Reformer" is contained in the sentences: "Every man ought to stand in primary relations with the work of the world; ought to do it himself, and not to suffer the accident of his having a purse in his pocket, or his having been bred to some dishonorable and injurious craft, to sever him from those duties. . . . Why needs any man be rich? Why must he have horses, fine garments, handsome apartments, access to public houses and places of amusement? Only for want of thought" (I, 229, 232); whereas the essay on "Wealth," published some twenty years later, is largely the elaboration of his opening contention that *every man* "is by constitution expensive, and needs to be rich" (VI, 85).

And again all this—one grows ashamed to say the same thing over so many times—means merely that property is justified or is not, according as the individual reaches his highest selfhood through it or by the want of it. "Do you complain of the laws of Property? It is pedantry to give such importance to them. Can we not play the game of life with these counters, as well as with those? in the institution of property, as well as out of it?" (III, 249).

With regard to all the institutions of society, therefore, the test is the highest good of the individual. Should the United States government be upheld when it is threatened by civil war? By all means. "It would be a pity to dissolve the Union and so diminish immensely every man's personal importance" (J. VI, 495). Then should its laws be sacred and implicitly followed? By no means! "Every actual state is corrupt. Good men must not obey the laws too well. . . . Any laws but those which men make for themselves are laughable" (III, 199, 205). And not only the state, but "the world exists for the education of each man. . . . He must sit solidly at home, and not suffer himself to be bullied by kings or empires, but know that he is greater than all the geography and all the government of the world" (II, 14).

Yet it is patent that "institutions are renovated only by combining independence and actual separateness" into some form of union (J. VI, 297); that while "the Spirit detaches you from all association" (p. 300), it is still the Spirit which "makes society possible" (II, 264); and hence while Emerson "will not sign a paper [and] abdicate my freedom" (J. III, 385), he fully recognizes the value of the community and of civilization, especially as it is this very thing which makes possible his independent way of living (J. II, 400); he recognizes that what is best for the individual is in reality "the good of all' (X, 183), that we earn our bread "by the hearty contribution of our energies to the common benefit" (I, 235), but the fundamental fact is always that "the union is only perfect when all the uniters are isolated. . . . Each man, if he attempts to join himself to others, is on all sides cramped and diminished of his proportion" (III, 253). If the individual wears the yoke of the multitude's opinion, then there is no more freedom in *this* tyranny than in that of kings.

That combining of men, therefore, which is instinctive in them, must go on, but must be for the sake of the individuals who make up the combination. It must never be for the sake of the product but for the sake of the producer only that a man should forfeit his right to "the amount of manual labor which is necessary to the maintenance of a family" (I, 230). "I would not have the laborer sacrificed to the result,—I would not have the laborer sacrificed to my convenience and pride, nor to that of a great class of such as me. Let there be worse cotton and better men" (I, 184). Nor should the man of letters or the philosopher separate himself from health-giving toil, even if this "indisposes and disqualifies for intellectual exertion. . . . Better that the book should not be quite so good, and the book-maker abler and better" (I, 230, 231).

The few passages in Emerson which have a socialistic cast are therefore just as individualistic as his most anarchistic statements. "If properties of this kind [music and works of art] were owned by states, towns, and lyceums, they would draw the bonds of neighborhood closer. . . . The public should step into the place of these [feudalistic European] proprietors, and provide this culture and inspiration for the citizen" (VI, 98). Emerson believes that there should be fair play and an open field— an equal scope for every creature (IV, 30); that in his highest stage man is devoted "no longer to the service of an individual, but to the common good of all men"; that we must not insist on such "coarse local distinctions as those of nation, province, or town" (V, 147); that "Society is barbarous until every industrious man can get his living without dishonest customs" (VI, 85); that "we make by distrust the thief, and burglar, and incendiary, and by our court and jail we keep him so" (I, 240) ; that therefore "the very prison [should be] compelled to maintain itself and yield a revenue, and, better still, made a reform school and a manufactory of honest men out of rogues" (VII, 29) ; that the unemployed poor cost as much in our taxes for poor-rates as if we paid them wages (VI, 108). But all these comments, which are the commonplaces of many a socialistic writer, are isolated expressions of a generous sentiment backed by an unwavering belief in the prime value of the individual man.

Emerson's inherent antagonism to all socialistic schemes of reform is best shown in considering his relation to the Brook Farm experiment. He wished "to be made nobly mad" by Ripley's appeal; and when he decided not to go into the association, it was, as he wrote to Ripley, "reluctantly, and I might almost say with penitence." But though he always extended his sympathy and was a frequent and most interested visitor, Emerson's whole philosophy was in opposition to the plan. There are too many references in the Journals and throughout his works and correspondence to include even a fair representation of the passages which illustrate his attitude toward Brook Farm; but it should now be fully apparent what his attitude would necessarily be. All that could surprise one is the delicious vein of humor running through almost all of these references.

When the earlier, idealistic period of Brook Farm was succeeded by the more formidable, overtly socialistic period,—that is, when the ideas of Fourier were taken over and Brook Farm became a "phalanx" in the universal system,—Emerson's tone changed from good-natured raillery to open hostility. Fourierism he calls "the sublime of mechanics" (X, 348) ; and when he says in other connections, "Souls are not saved in bundles" (VI, 205), or "Our society is encumbered by ponderous machinery" (II, 130), he is showing the same attitude that he always held regarding all forcing of the individual by artificial means. In an article in *The Dial* for July, 1842, entitled "Fourierism and the Socialists," [112] he says on behalf of those who opposed the change at Brook Farm: "Our feeling was that Fourier had skipped no fact but one, namely, Life." Couldn't Fourier know, he asks, a little farther on, that "a similar model lay in every mind, and that the method of each associate might be trusted, as well as that of his particular committee?" And in the lecture on "New England Reformers," after stating somewhat ironically the purpose of such communities, he continues: "Yet it may easily be questioned . . . whether such a retreat does not promise to become an asylum to those who have tried and failed, rather than a field to the strong; and

---

[112] Republished in *Uncollected Writings*. N. Y.: The Lamb Pub. Co.

whether the members will not necessarily be fractions of men, because each finds that he cannot enter it without some compromise. Friendship and association are very fine things, and a grand phalanx of the best of the human race, banded for some catholic object; yes, excellent; but remember that no society can ever be so large as one man. He, in his friendship, in his natural and momentary associations, doubles or multiplies himself; but in the hour in which he mortgages himself to two or ten or twenty, he dwarfs himself beyond the stature of one" (III, 251).

I trust that what I have said sufficiently indicates that it was not his lack of human sentiment, his aloofness and coldness, that kept Emerson out of the Brook Farm association, but rather the fundamental consistency of his thought. But does this answer as well for his isolation and apparent indifference regarding the other reform movements of the time? We can scarcely claim that. For was not the greatest of all—the freeing of the slaves—due largely to the very Emersonian determination to give the black man the chance to develop his independent individuality? Did not the temperance advocates endeavor to place other enslaved individuals in command of themselves? Were not those earliest stirrings on behalf of "women's rights" quite as much for the freedom of the individual? And was not this the case as well with other movements with which so many of Emerson's associates were identified?

In the first place, Emerson did not remain apart from the practical work of the world to anything like the extent that he is sometimes accused of doing. He attended the first national convention held for the political emancipation of women; he attended town meetings and debated in a most interested way on good roads, honest tax collection, the distribution of public money, and the faithful performance of public service;[113] and so closely did he finally become associated with the antislavery movement that Chapman says he sent ten thousand sons to the war.

But Emerson was never an agitator, and with reason. His fellow Transcendentalists were for the most part swept off their feet by the various appeals of the time; but to have been moved as they were would have shown in Emerson no fundamental conviction in his main beliefs. For if the things which called for reform in politics and in civilization itself should move us to rage and despair, are we not impeaching the divine order, and losing faith in the great evolving moral law? Carlyle saw the variableness of appearance, for all his railing against our concerning ourselves with the "surfaces" of things, until he seemed to become blinded to the underlying unity of the eternal Good, and this re-

[113] Minot J. Savage, in the New York *Tribune* for May 25, 1903.

sulted in his pronounced pessimism; but Emerson never lost his hold on
what to him were the fundamentals. Somehow, he felt, these horrors
which we see must come into accord with the scheme of things, and *that*
must never be scattered and identified with them.

Thus Carlyle writes to Emerson:[114] "You seem to me in danger of
dividing yourselves [the editors of *The Dial*] from the fact of this present universe, in which alone, ugly as it is, can I find any anchorage, and
soaring away after Ideas, Beliefs, Revelations, and such like,—into peril-
ous altitudes as I think. . . . It is the whole Past and the whole Future,
this same cotton-spinning, dollar-hunting, canting and shrieking, very
wretched generation of ours. Come back into it, I tell you." And Emerson answers, somewhat later:[115] "Of what you say now and heretofore
respecting the remoteness of my writing and thinking from real life
. . . I do not know what it means. If I can at any time express the law
and the ideal right, that should satisfy me without measuring the diver-
gence from it of the last act of Congress." And in an earlier letter,
written when the fervor of his philosophic impulse was at its height,[116]
Emerson says: "My whole philosophy—which is very real—teaches ac-
quiescence and optimism."

That, therefore, which restrained Emerson from rushing into this
and the other reform, was primarily his firm belief that "the whole frame
of things preaches indifferency" (III, 62); "that a higher law than that
of our will regulates events; that our painful labors are unnecessary and
fruitless" (II, 132); "that there is no need of struggles, convulsions, and
despairs, of the wringing of the hands and the gnashing of the teeth;
that we miscreate our own evils. . . . Nature will not have us fret and
fume. She does not like our benevolence or our learning much better
than she likes our frauds and wars. When we come out of the caucus,
or the bank, or the Abolition-convention, or the Temperance-meeting, or
the Transcendental club into the fields and woods, she says to us, "So
hot? my little Sir'" (II, 129).

It cannot be denied that this bland optimism is somewhat maddening at times, when one feels deeply the need of definite and aggressive
action. It is small comfort, when one is smarting under the injustice of
certain special conditions, to be told that "it is only the finite that has
wrought and suffered; the infinite lies stretched in smiling repose"
(II, 126)! But this is Emerson's first answer to the charge of indifferency to practical duties. "As soon as a man is wonted to look beyond

---

[114] *Correspondence*, vol. II, pp. 11, 12.

[115] *Ib.*, p. 85.

[116] 31 July, 1841. *Correspondence*, vol. I, p. 367.

surfaces, and to see how this high will prevails without an exception or an interval, he settles himself into serenity. . . . We need not assist the administration of the universe" (III, 269). But the other side of this matter was too obvious for Emerson to be wholly blind to it: While "the solar system has no anxiety about its reputation" (VI, 194), we must somewhat concern ourselves with our own reputations; and although "there is a tendency in things to right themselves" (VI, 242), yet on the other hand "the fact that I am here certainly shows me that the Soul has need of an organ here" (II, 154). The individual cannot realize himself without reacting properly upon his environment:

> "Freedom's secret wilt thou know?
> Right thou feelest, rush to do" (VI, 204).

Inasmuch, then, as "the sentiment never stops in pure vision, but will be enacted" (X, 104), and "our duty requires us to be the very hands of this guiding sentiment and work in the present moment," we cannot make Emerson's optimistic belief that things will come out right in the end equivalent to a mere fatalistic doctrine of *laissez-faire,* but we must seek farther for the full explanation of his neglect of much that he might apparently have done. There is something to be said by way of extenuation in what Professor James called "his fidelity to the limits of his genius;" [117] and Emerson himself freely admits from time to time that he would gladly have performed more and greater tasks. He records feeling a sense of shame and guilt at his avoidance of the appeals of temperance, anti-slavery, etc., but adds: "I cannot do all these things, but these my shames are illustrious token that I have strict relations to them all" (J. IV, 371); and moreover, the "good intention, which seems so cheap beside this brave zeal, is the back-bone of the world" (J. IV, 301). Like Mary, the optimistic sister of the industrious Martha, Emerson chose the better part for himself. But he does not deceive himself with this self-exoneration. It is easy and pleasant to lecture on anti-slavery, he tells himself in his Journal, and leave someone else to do your duty at home (J. VI, 534)!

At times Emerson does seem to place his own individuality above the more generous call of service to humanity; he seems to be an individualist at the expense of others. With delightful humor he puts this reversal of conventional altruism in favor of an almost Nietzschean self-assertion: "I once asked a clergyman in a retired town, who were his companions? what men of ability he saw? He replied that he spent his time with the sick and the dying. I said he seemed to me to need quite

[117] *Memories and Studies,* p. 23.

other company" (VI, 250)! The essay on Friendship exhibits something
of this same attitude.   There should be small consideration for the feel-
ings of the friend, he teaches by implication, if the friendship jeopardizes
one's own intellectual independence; or, as Professor L. W. Smith, in
comparing Emerson with Ibsen and Nietzsche, expresses this type of individualism, "One must not permit himself to be materially hindered by
consideration for others." [118] "One would think," says Vernon Lee, "were
it not for the evidence of a hundred scattered utterances of most deli-
cate loving-kindness, that Emerson was a fierce intellectual egotist like
Abelard." [119]   But no one who has read and loved his Emerson could
seriously think of him as other than most generous, most considerate and
kind, however much his personal selfhood might need defense from the
multifarious appeals of this and that reform.   Only, the individual must
not be lost in the issue.   The test is, "if we keep our independence, yet
do not lose our sympathy" (VI, 20).   By all means let us have reform
when it educates the individual (VII, 28, 29).   But we must not be
swept out of our own orbit.   And we must conserve our strength; who
would deny that?   "A man's income is not sufficient for all things.   If
he spends here, he must save there" (J. IV, 301).

But in the case of anti-slavery Emerson encountered a reform which
dwarfed the pretensions of any individual.   Here was an appeal which no
thoughtful citizen could escape; and it was particularly urgent upon one
who made freedom the last reach of the soul's progress.   Mere freedom
from physical fetters was of course of the least consequence.   "I have
quite other slaves to free than these negroes," he wrote in his Journal as
late as 1852, "to wit, imprisoned thoughts far back in the minds of men."
And more openly, in his "Lecture on the Times," in 1841: "How trivial
seem the contests of the abolitionist, whilst he aims merely at the circumstance of the slave.   Give the slave the least elevation of religious sentiment, and he is no slave" (I, 266).   But it were sophistry and the most
foolish of paradoxes to pretend that liberty was not better both for the
individual and the race than bondage could ever be; and Emerson knew
well enough that, however superior to circumstance he might hold himself, he could no more dodge this issue than the most matter-of-fact of
his comrades.   He knew at first hand the horrors of slavery from his
stay in South Carolina and Florida, in 1826; he was humane by nature;
and never the least afraid of that hostility and opprobrium which silenced
many a northern minister who would otherwise have spoken on behalf
of freedom.   During his incumbency at Second Church, Boston, from

---

[118] *Popular Science Monthly,* LXXVIII, 149.
[119] *Contemporary Review,* LXVII, 348.

1829 to 1833, he opened his church freely to anti-slavery meetings, which was then an heroic—almost a desperate—thing to do. "Waldo invited me to be his guest in the midst of my unpopularity," writes Harriet Martineau, referring to the stormy year of 1836. "He has spoken more abundantly and boldly, the more critical the times became." [120] And indeed there is nothing more interesting in the Journals than the record of Emerson's growing response to the call of the Abolitionists.

One other consideration may be mentioned, though this applies to Emerson's attitude toward reforms of all kinds and not to anti-slavery in particular. "His objection to all reform," says Professor Woodberry, "which he always looked at dubiously in the concrete, was its partial and particular nature." [121] Emerson himself puts it much more strongly: "He who aims at progress should aim at an infinite, not at a special benefit. . . . There is no end to which your practical faculty can aim, so sacred and so large, that, if pursued for itself, will not at last become carrion and an offense to the nostril" (I, 205).

Therefore, when Emerson says, "I cannot afford to be irritable and captious, nor to waste all my time in attacks" (III, 249), he is not so much excusing himself as accusing his friends. "The Reform of Reforms," he writes, "must be accomplished without means. . . . I think the work of the reformer as innocent as any other work that is done around him; but when I have seen it near, I do not like it better. It is done in the same way, it is done profanely, not piously; by management, by tactics and clamor. It is a buzz in the ear" (I, 263, 264). Now there are two ways of reforming men: by force, and by persuasion; by law, and by precept; by coercion, and by love. Emerson has the temerity to propose to us in all seriousness that "the way to mend the bad world is to create the right world" (VI, 214); that our task is "to tend to the correction of flagrant wrongs by laying one stone aright every day" (I, 235); that "the remedy for all blunders, the cure of blindness, the cure of crime, is love" (VI, 208). "The power of love, as the basis of a State," he says with charming naïveté, "has never been tried" (III, 209).

Regarding the freeing of the slaves, therefore, Emerson long held to the hope that this good might come by the force of love instead of through hatred and murder—as who would not? If only the slave-owners would realize—as surely they soon must—how desirable freedom would be for the slave, and how beneficial to their own souls the granting of it, they must inevitably release these groping seekers after liberty; and how much better that would be than if they were compelled to relinquish the

---

[120] *Autobiography*, vol. I, p. 375.
[121] *Ralph Waldo Emerson*, p. 69.

slaves against their will! "To wish for war is atheism" he writes in his Journal (J. VI, 203), and he determined that he would "confide to the end in spiritual not in carnal weapons" (J. VI, 104). It is true that when war had become a necessity, he admitted that "there are times when gunpowder smells good," and his optimism triumphed in the reflection that the unawakened man might find. great benefits from it: "If war with his cannonade . . . can set his dull nerves throbbing, and by loud taps on the tough chrysalis can break its walls and let the new creature emerge erect and free,—make way and sing pæan" (VI, 158). But this was merely taking the bull by the horns. So far as he has any theory regarding the relation of the individual to the work of practical reform, it seems to be that one should make of himself a shining example; let him love his neighbor; and then all men, according to their own possibilities, would work out their individual salvations, the Spirit determining that this must be in the right direction and to a perfect accomplishment in course of time. "Let the soul be erect and all things will go well." "Whenever I find my dominion over myself not sufficient for me, and undertake the direction of [my neighbor] also, I overstep the truth, and come into false relations with him" (III, 204). "This is the remedy for all ills, the panacea of nature. We must be lovers and at once the impossible becomes possible. . . . Let our affection flow out to our fellows; it would operate in a day the greatest of all revolutions. . . . Let the amelioration of our laws of property proceed from the concession of the rich, not from the grasping of the poor" (I, 239). The "rich young man" was advised to sell all he had and give to the poor, and Emerson would consider the advice eminently practical; no doubt it was,—but still the young man "went away sorrowful." Emerson's prescription for the world's woes did not really differ from that of Jesus. "He taught us how to live," says Edward Everett Hale;[122] "and he did so because he lived himself"—in which, as in other ways, he reminds us of Chaucer's Parson. Theodore Parker "flung himself, sword in hand, into the thick of the conflict," says James Freeman Clarke;[123] "but . . . the power of Emerson to soften the rigidity of time-hardened belief was far the greater. It is the old fable of the storm and the sun." And so far as Emerson did enter into the conflict, that is to be accounted for by a sentence in one of his letters to Sterling.[124] "The problems of reform" he wrote, as far back as 1840, "are losing their local and sectarian character, and becoming generous, profound, and poetic."

---

[122] *Op. cit.*, p. 258.
[123] *Nineteenth Century Questions*, p. 247.
[124] *Correspondence*, p. 31.

It would need no ghost new risen from the ground to tell us that there was one reform to which Emerson could give himself with complete consistency. "What we call our root-and-branch reforms," he says, "of slavery, war, gambling, intemperance, is only medicating the symptoms. We must begin higher up, namely, in Education" (VI, 136). Immediately after his little book, *Nature,* Emerson gave his magnificent address on "The American Scholar," so justly called by Holmes "our intellectual Declaration of Independence;" and his later lecture on "Education" (X, 123-156), says Edwin D. Mead, "is the most vital, pregnant and stimulating word upon general education which has been written by an American." In both cases Emerson's purpose is constructive reform,—in the first instance fundamental, in the second more specific. In these, as in the many other passages where the matter of education is touched upon, Emerson regards education as "the only sure means of permanent and progressive reform"—to quote the words of President Emeritus Eliot.[125] Indeed, our whole consideration of this subject could lead us to no other conclusion. "His message, therefore," says Kuno Francke, "while fully accepting Fichte's appeal for self-surrender of private interests to public purposes, culminated not in the demand of concentration, but in the demand of expansion of the individual." [126] And what means for this expansion of the individual is there other than by substituting for the present cramping and confining system of education a wise, all-round, and "natural" method?

There is no need for an analysis of Emerson's theory of education. What he has said on this subject is not cryptic but perfectly open and clear, and there are no apparent inconsistencies to be resolved. One has only to read the lecture on "Education" to fit its various contentions into the general scheme of Emerson's thinking which has now been analyzed with some fulness. And such other notes as one finds in the Journals, the Correspondence, and the collected Works only substantiate these views.

One question, however, might be asked: How is Emerson's insistence upon the necessity of manual labor and scientific and technical training as a basis for education consistent with his belief that "the spirit only can teach" (I, 132)? On the one hand he anticipates Horace Mann in some of his definite and practical reforms; on the other he derives from Pestalozzi (whom he frequently quotes in his Journal), in believing that "no man is able or willing to help any other man" (J. II, 483), since "every man must learn in a different way," namely, by self-education, and

125 *Atlantic Monthly,* XCI: 846.
126 *German Ideals of To-Day,* p. 119.

"in reality there is no other" (p. 521). But it would be a wilful bor-
rowing of trouble to find any essential difficulty here. The development
of all a man's faculties is in a way a mechanical means of expanding
his personality and of making him more capable of receiving truth from
above. " 'Tis inhuman to want faith in the power of education, since to
ameliorate is the law of nature" (VI, 135) ; but at the same time "we
feel that a man's talents stand in the way of his advancement in truth"
(II, 270)—when they are cultivated for their own sake. On the practical side, "Education makes man prevail over circumstance" (J. V,
441) ; on the spiritual side the object of education is to remove obstruc-
tions and let natural force have free play (J. III, 416).

Hence the trouble with our colleges is that they "foster an eminent
talent in any youth. If he refuse prayers and recitations, they will tor-
ment and traduce and expel him, though he were a Newton or Dante"
(J. VII, 56). There is too much machinery in our educational system;
we lose the central reality and graduate a dunce (J. III, 275). So
strongly does Emerson insist upon the superiority of instinct over culture
(XII, 34), of genius over talent (II, 270), which are alike merely the
transcendence of the "Reason" over the "Understanding," that one sometimes feels, with Sadler,[127] that he neglected the side of discipline; and
indeed to *impose* discipline, even upon a child, did seem to Emerson a
going beyond one's just prerogative. The child, he always believed,
would instruct the teacher as to the best method of procedure, and this,
of course, could never be by coercion. But accuracy, system, drill,—
these were by no means omitted from Emerson's educational scheme. To
each he pauses to render tribute (X, 145; VI, 114; VI, 77) ; but these
were always secondary, obvious, and not in need of special emphasis.
He notes the disciplinary value of mathematics and the languages; it is
only when they ceased to have any "strict relation to science and culture"
and "became stereotyped as Education" (J. VI, 289), that he objects to
their crowding out of more vital and practical subjects.

---

[127] *Educational Review*, XXVI: 459.

CHAPTER X.

EMERSON'S ESTHETICS: THE MEANING OF BEAUTY; THE UTILITY OF ART.

It is rather surprising that Emerson should have so little of value to offer us by way of an esthetic theory, since he was primarily a poet, and his idealism was a complete system which reached into all the essential divisions of philosophy. What his esthetic theory would necessarily be has already become apparent to anyone (if there is any such person!) who has read thus far in this essay. This is a tribute to Emerson's fundamental consistency, but not to the depth of his thinking. One could not read the *Critique of Pure Reason* and the *Critique of Pure Practical Reason,* and then produce the *Critique of Judgment,* however consistent a part it may be of the Critical Philosophy. But Emerson's basic doctrine of Intuition and his Puritanical ancestry predetermined all he had to say regarding the meaning of beauty and the utility of art.

Emerson's ideas regarding beauty and art are among the first to find expression in his Journals. But even earlier than the theory are the critical judgments which are the logical if anticipatory conclusions of that theory, and they are not modified as the theory becomes formulated. He asserts that Wordsworth's "noble distinction is that he seeks the truth" (J. II, 430); whereas he is "frigid to the Byrons" (J. IV, 324), Tennyson he regards as "a beautiful half of a poet," [128] and to Shelley he refers so frequently and with such animosity that it would seem he entertained a religious aversion to all "art for art's sake." Later he becomes more tolerant: Shelley is good for others, so must not be overlooked, and Tennyson is good by one test—that he has a "liberating" effect on us (J. VI, 115, 218). It is the same with his judgment of fiction. At the age of twenty-one he writes in his Journal that one portion of the world's literature "seems specially intended for coxcombs and deficient persons. To this department belong the greatest part of Novels and Romances" (J. II, 13). Scott's *Bride of Lammermoor* appealed to him because of the nobility and symbolic significance of the characters (J. II, 371), whereas he was angry at having become so interested in *Quentin Durward* that he read it through; he "had been duped and dragged after a foolish boy and girl, to see them at last married and portioned, and I in-

---

[128] Letter to Furness, 1838, in the latter's *Records of a Lifelong Friendship,* p. 7.

stantly turned out of doors." Had one noble thought, one sentiment of God been spoken by them, he felt that he would not have been thus excluded (J. V, 515). Dickens succeeds because "monstrous exaggeration is an easy secret of romance" (J. VI, 312), and all "antiques"—as those of Landor, Goethe, Coleridge, Scott—are "paste jewels" (J. VI, 400). His judgment is the same regarding all the arts. Let one striking instance stand for the rest. Speaking of the ballet between the acts at a certain performance he reflects that "Goethe laughs at who can't admire a picture as a picture. So I looked and admired, but felt it were better for mankind if there were no such dancers;" and he feels, moreover, that God agrees, since most of them are nearly idiotic (J. III, 113)!

These estimates of literature and the other arts would have been exactly what they are though Emerson had never had a philosophic or esthetic theory. Indeed, Emerson could not in sincerity have formulated any system of esthetics which would not have yielded just such results as these, however logically consistent it might have been. These, to him, were the facts; and the test of any theory was that it should explain the facts (I, 10). What, then, does Emerson believe must be the underlying basis of truth of which these facts are the outcroppings?

Emerson attempts no definition of beauty, warned, he says, by the failure of many philosophers who have attempted it (VI, 274); but no modern thinker, says Morley, makes so much of the place of beauty in the scheme of things.[129] This is because he regards beauty as the truest revelation of the mystery of nature.[130] "In the eternal trinity of Truth, Goodness, and Beauty, each in its perfection including the three, [the Transcendentalists] prefer to make Beauty the sign and head. . . . We call the Beautiful the highest, because it appears to us the golden mean, escaping the dowdiness of the good and the heartlessness of the true" (I, 334, 335). "The new virtue which constitutes a thing beautiful is a certain cosmical quality, or a power to suggest relation to the whole world, and so lift the object out of a pitiful individuality. Every natural feature,—sea, sky, rainbow, flowers, musical tone—has in it somewhat which is not private but universal, speaks of that central benefit which is the soul of Nature, and thereby is beautiful. . . . All beauty points at identity. . . . Into every beautiful object there enters somewhat immeasurable and divine . . . Beauty hiding all wisdom and power in its calm sky" (VI, 287-290).

The perception of such Beauty is of course an act of the Intuition, and

---

[129] *Crit. Misc.*, vol. I, p. 330.

[130] See "The Poems of Emerson" by C. C. Everett, in *Essays Theological and Literary*.

its contemplation belongs to the Reason and not to the Understanding. "Every man parts from that contemplation [of the universal and eternal beauty] with the feeling that it rather belongs to ages than to mortal life" (II, 256). From this comes its ethical relationship, and from that in turn its practical utility when embodied in the form of art. From the very start Emerson insists upon this aspect of it: "Beauty is the mark God sets upon virtue" (I, 25); and to this aspect of it he constantly returns: "All high beauty has a moral element in it, and I find the antique sculpture as ethical as Marcus Antoninus" (VI, 290).

It follows that "nothing is quite beautiful alone; nothing but is beautiful in the whole. A single object is only so far beautiful as it suggests this universal grace. . . . The world thus exists to the soul to satisfy the desire of beauty" (I, 29). In its last analysis, Emerson regards this perception of the beauty of the totality of things as an ethical and religious matter, though he sometimes speaks of it more humanly as an act of reflection, of thought, or even by the esthetically technical term "imagination." "When the act of reflection takes place in the mind," he says somewhat vaguely, "when we look at ourselves in the light of thought, we discover that our life is embosomed in beauty" (II, 125). "Things are pretty, graceful, rich, elegant, handsome, but, until they speak to the imagination, not yet beautiful" (VI, 287). But the imagination which creates this final beauty as an interpretation of the universe is just as necessary in order to perceive any individual object as beautiful; and this is only another way of saying that "not in nature but in man is all the beauty he sees" (II, 140). Every schoolboy has noticed that. The squeak of a bicycle on a lonely road mistaken for the note of a bird in the bushes was piercingly beautiful until it was recognized, when it became piercingly annoying. Yet it remained the same sound. A philosopher who finds the primary qualities of objects existent in the perceiving mind need not register his conviction that beauty does not exist in the things themselves. This familiar discovery, which Emerson seems to have first found stated in 1823—"The theory of Mr. Alison, assigning the beauty of the object to the mind of the beholder, is natural and plausible" (J. II, 304)—he connected definitely with his idealism: "We animate what we see, and we see only what we animate. . . . It depends on the mood of the man whether he shall see the sunset or the fine poem" (III, 54).

In his poems, particularly in the "Ode to Beauty," Emerson develops these and kindred ideas, but I find no new phases of his thinking in them. "Each and All' is perhaps his best statement of the thought that the individual object gets its beauty from its relation to the whole. But without discounting the high value of this and many other poems of Emerson, one may still look to his prose for the most adequate account of his actual thinking. This is the more remarkable inasmuch as Emerson holds that "Poetry preceded prose as Reason, whose vehicle poetry is, precedes the Understanding" (J. III, 492) ; and he constantly speaks of the poet as the inspired bringer of truth to men. But this is using poetry in its largest sense; it is identifying poetic inspiration with all mystical intuition,—as Emerson frankly does. "This is Instinct, and Inspiration is only this power excited, breaking its silence" (XII, 32).

Now as "Instinct," as he is here calling it, "has a range as wide as human nature, running all over the ground of morals, of intellect, and of sense" (XII, 33), so "the poet, like the electric rod, must reach from a point nearer the sky than all surrounding objects, down to the earth, and into the dark wet soil" (XII, 226). There is nothing new about this conception of the man of genius as the mediator between the highest and the most commonplace, except the mystical coloring which Emerson gives it. On the one hand, "when it [the Over-Soul] breathes through his intellect, it is genius" (II, 255) ; on the other hand, "to believe that what is true for you in your private heart is true for all men,—that is genius" (II, 47). By the doctrine of Intuition, as has been noted earlier in this essay, all men may enter into a first-hand relationship with the source of wisdom; but there are many who prefer to dwell on the lower levels and who must therefore learn of the finer spirits who yield themselves to the reception of truth. It is the converse of the same matter to say, "What are these millions who read and behold, but incipient writers and sculptors? Add a little more to that quality which now reads and sees, and they will seize the pen and chisel," and "Common sense . . . is the basis of genius, and experience is hands and feet to every enterprise; and yet," Emerson hastens to add, "he who should do his business on this understanding would be quickly bankrupt" (III, 68, 69).

Emerson's doctrine of inspiration differs from Plato's, as brought out in the *Ion* and elsewhere, only in its greater insistence upon the practical usefulness of the message and in that the "some god" of Socrates becomes definitely the Over-Soul itself. To Plato he is careful to attribute the thought that "poets utter great and wise things which they do not themselves understand" (II, 37), which he has paraphrased in the familiar lines from "The Problem,"

> "He builded better than he knew;
> The conscious stone to beauty grew."

But this, like the ethical purpose of poetry, is with Emerson, as with Plato, a mere corollary of the inspiration theory.

His fellow Transcendentalists shared with Emerson his belief in inspiration, but did not always share his saving sense of humor. Jones Very, sending some of his poems and essays to Emerson, wrote, "I am glad to transmit what has been told me of Shakespeare. You hear not mine own words, but the teaching of the Holy Ghost." [131] Emerson escapes such egotism by making his statements of this sort impersonal—"All writing comes by the grace of God" (III, 71)—and by fully recognizing that the individual does not cease to be himself when he is the recipient of a revelation. Indeed, he goes so far as to say, "To believe your own thought, that is Genius" (J. IV, 55), "A meek self-reliance I believe to be the law and constitution of good writing" (J. III, 550), and "What we say, however trifling, must have its roots in ourselves, or it will not move others" (J. II, 505).

"Genius" therefore "is religious," *because* "it is a larger imbibing of the common heart. It is not anomalous, but more like and not less like other men. There is in all great poets a wisdom of humanity which is superior to any talents they exercise" (II, 270). Hence it is no contradiction for this believer in mystical inspiration to say, "If you would learn to write, 'tis in the street you must learn it" (VII, 16). The bringer of the message must resolve in himself the dualism between the truth he receives and the people to whom he gives it, by identifying himself both with the original giver and the last receiver. "A painter told me that nobody could draw a tree without in some sort becoming a tree" (II, 21); and on the other hand, "Perhaps, if we should meet Shakespeare we should not be conscious of any steep inferiority; no, but of a great equality,—only that he possessed a strange skill of using, or classifying his facts, which we lacked. For notwithstanding our utter incapacity to produce anything like Hamlet and Othello, see the perfect reception this wit and immense knowledge of life and liquid eloquence find in us all" (II, 310).

This is no more than to say, when we bring it down to the terms of literary criticism, that idealism is the method of all art,—that the subject must pass through the writer's or artist's personality,—only Emerson insists that since intuition is an act of piety the man of genius must necessarily be a "pious" man. At the age of twenty-three he mentions piety as one of the attributes of the "genuine bard" (J. II, 106); and before he is yet twenty he finds that there is a "tendency in the passions" which "seems to consist in the pleasure of finding out a connection between a material image and a moral sentiment" (J. I, 105). One would think that a man who took so didactic a view of art would be narrow beyond

---

[131] Cooke's *Poets of Transcendentalism*, p. 12.

belief in his literary and artistic judgments; but though Emerson is somewhat blind to the sheer beauty of such a man as Shelley, no one ever had a finer appreciation of the glory which is Shakespeare. This is somewhat because of Emerson's recognition of Shakespeare's supreme art— "his principal merit is that he can say what he will" (IV, 19)—but much more because Emerson could not avoid putting such an ethical interpretation upon whatever appealed to him that he instinctively gave the most Christian coloring to the most pagan of men. One often smiles at his bundling together of some half-dozen worthies who were as far separated spiritually as they were historically. Misery never made such strange bedfellows as have been brought together by Emerson's glowing admiration. But while his taste was so catholic, his ethical interpretation of art was not compromised. "Shakespeare, Herrick, Jonson . . . suggest the endowment of spiritual men" to such an extent that "Dante, Tasso, Wordsworth are pale beside them" (J. II, 236) ! Emerson in the voice of Genius hears always the moral tone even when it is "disowned in words" (X, 179). In saying "Only that is poetry which cleanses and mans me" (J. V, 402), he is saying not only that art is ethical but also that he is able to get an ethical reaction out of some poetry which has a purely esthetic value for others. It is strange that he remained obdurate to the call of Shelley, who has so high an ethical appeal to some who take even Shakespeare on a purely human level.

According to Emerson, then, beauty is that which inheres in the idea or object to be imitated, and art is the expression which genius is able to give to it. While beauty is perceived by the Reason, art must be wrought under the guidance of the Understanding. Emerson emphasizes the divine rather than the human aspect of art, and thus he feels that not imitation, even in Aristotle's large meaning of the term, but creation is the aim of art (II, 327). For art cannot directly imitate beauty, since the Understanding cannot perceive at first hand what is revealed only to the Reason: "Go forth to find it [beauty], and it is gone; 'tis only a mirage as you look from the windows of diligence" (J. III, 556); but "certain minds, more closely harmonized with nature, possess the power of abstracting Beauty from things, and reproducing it in new forms. . . . This is art" (XII, 118).

Since "the office of art [is] to educate the perception of beauty" (II, 329), it follows that the principles of art are to be deduced from the nature of beauty. It is because "Beauty, in its largest and profoundest sense, is one expression for the universe" (I, 30) that "Art should . . . throw down the walls of circumstance on every side, awakening in the beholder the same sense of universal relation" (II, 338); it is because beauty "involves a moral charm" (VI, 207) that "the high poetry of the world from its beginning has been ethical" (J. IV, 425) ; it is because "Beauty rests on necessities" (VI, 279), and "what is most real is most beautiful" (XII, 117), that it is "idle to choose a random sparkle here or there" (VI, 51), and that when "lively boys write to their ear and eye, the cool reader finds nothing but sweet jingles in it" (III, 223) ; it is because "everything is a monster till we know what it is for . . . and then the thing tells its story at sight and is beautiful" (J. II, 489) that "our taste in building . . . refuses pilasters and columns that support nothing, and allows the real supporters of the house honestly to show themselves" (VI, 276).

Emerson, then, is to be numbered among those who reduce beauty to terms of utility and adaptability, at least so far as beauty appears in the form of art. Conversely, whatever is adequate to its purpose must necessarily be beautiful, and consequently Emerson anticipates Kipling in saying that the locomotive is not prosaic but highly poetic (J. VI, 336), and he finds that "the aesthetic value of railroads is to unite the advantages of town and country life" (VI, 142). It is true that Beauty is a "nobler want" of man than mere commodity, (I, 21), and that "a man is a beggar who lives only to the useful" (VI, 152) ; but the utility must still be there, however much Emerson may say in his little poem, "The Rhodora," that "Beauty is its own excuse for being." Of course the highest utility is ethical, and when beauty seems most remote from the practical it may be nearest to the spiritual. "The critics who complain of the sickly separation of the beauty of nature from the thing to be done, must consider that our hunting of the picturesque is inseparable from our protest against false society" (VI, 275). But the advantages to be gained from art are often merely practical and useful. "I think sculpture and painting have an effect to teach us manners and abolish hurry" (VI, 153) ; and "novels are as useful as Bibles if they teach you the secret that the best of life is conversation, and the greatest success is confidence, or perfect understanding between sincere people" (VI, 184).

When, therefore, beauty is separated from utility it ceases to be beautiful. "Nothing merely ornamental can be beautiful" (J. IV, 88) ; indeed Emerson goes so far as to say that "outside embellishment is deformity" (VI, 275). Applied in the province of literary criticism this leads him to say, "Don't affect the use of an adverb or an epithet more than belongs to the feeling you have" (J. II, 427), for "the positive is the sinew of speech, the superlative the fat" (X, 160). But it does not follow that a work of art should be bare and stupid. "Beauty without grace is the hook without the bait" (VI, 284), and dullness in a genius "is as insupportable as any other dullness" (J. VI, 359).

Emerson was much more sensible to beauty in the human form and in nature than he is generally accredited with being. This is evidenced in the Journals [132] more directly and positively than in the works which have always been familiar, and the publication of the Journals may in time correct this as well as other false impressions regarding him. But Emerson did not, apparently, feel any antagonism between sensuous charm and moral beauty; or rather, he felt that the separation was arbitrary and temporary, and one which the soul must readjust. "Whilst thus the world will be whole and refuses to be disparted, we seek to act partially, to sunder, to appropriate; for example,—to gratify the senses we sever the pleasure of the senses from the needs of the character. The ingenuity of man has always been dedicated to the solution of one problem,—how to detach the sensual sweet, the sensual strong, the sensual bright, etc., from the moral sweet, the moral deep, the moral fair. . . . The soul strives amain to live and work through all things. . . . This dividing and detaching is steadily counteracted. . . . Pleasure is taken out of pleasant things . . . as soon as we seek to separate them from the whole" (II, 100, 101). Browning's "Nor soul helps flesh more, now, than flesh helps soul" must have appeared to Emerson as the statement of an axiom. He could scarcely have seen why Plato's two horses did not trot amiably side by side along the highway.

I think it is this which prevents Emerson's esthetics from being more than a mere offshoot from his ethics. He does not grapple with any of the essential problems or throw any new light upon them. The pleasure to be derived from the tragic, for example, or the place of ugliness in art, are questions which do not exist for him. In his essay on "The Tragic" he says blithely: "There are people who have an appetite for grief. . . . They mis-hear and mis-behold. . . . All sorrow dwells in a low region. It is superficial; for the most part fantastic, or in the appearance and not in things" (XII, 265). And in his essay on "The Poet": "For as it is dislocation and detachment from the life of God that makes things ugly, the poet, who re-attaches things to nature and the Whole, . . . disposes very easily of the most disagreeable facts" (III, 23). Of course he recognzes the use that art makes of tragic material: "Art lives and thrills in new use and combining of contrasts, and mining into the dark evermore for blacker pits of night. What would painter do, or what would poet or saint, but for crucifixions and hells? And evermore in the world is this marvelous balance of beauty and disgust,

---

[132] See, for example, J. V., 118.

magnificence and rats" (VI, 242). But this makes no contribution whatever to the underlying problems of the tragic and the ugly.

There seems to be no way of establishing the relative value of a poet, and everyone remarks that comparisons in this kind are particularly odious. But since Matthew Arnold shocked all Boston by asserting that Emerson, upon whom he places the highest of values, was still neither philosopher nor poet, and this has passed by his authority into something of a tradition, I may be pardoned for setting beside it three opinions on the other side. Hermann Grimm regarded Emerson as "the greatest of all living authors;" Theodore Parker gives him "the highest place since Milton;" and Alexander Ireland, who quotes these judgments, says, "When the world is wiser, Emerson will be owned as a great poet." [133] Why should I not also indulge in the luxury of an opinion? From a fairly careful reading of the major American poets, I venture the judgment that Emerson, while not a great poet in the strictest sense, should rank with Whitman and Poe as one of the three best that this country has produced. His distinguishing excellences are the height and depth of his thought, the perfect sincerity through which he reveals the charm of his personality, and at times his remarkable response to the beauty of nature. His chief limitations lie in the narrowness of his range, and in the haltingness of his meter and mechanical monotony of his rhyme, giving to much of his work an appearance of amateurishness of which the most minor of poets would be ashamed. And it is a proof of his authenticity as a poet that we should instantly feel that if the babblings of these bardlings were found on his pages, instead of enhancing his value they would actually detract from Emerson's standing as a poet.

To a certain extent, the limitations I have mentioned are due to Emerson's being, as Professor Woodberry calls him, "a poet of imperfect faculty." To a much greater extent I believe they are the direct result of his esthetic theory, and that the value of that theory may somewhat be tested by the poetry it produced. For it must be remembered that, from the standpoint of technique, Emerson's early verses as a rule far surpass his later and greater poems. There is not a halting line in the tentative efforts at verse making given in the Journals till we reach about the year 1834 and the poems which he chose later to include in his collection. With a more perfect gift of utterance no doubt he would have conveyed his thought as well as he does without putting any strain upon his art; but when, as often happens with the best of poets, there was a conflict between art and thought,—the idea being precisely *this* and meter or rhyme suggesting a circumlocution to *that,*—Emerson never hesitated to

---

[133] *In Memoriam: Ralph Waldo Emerson,* pp. 32, 37, 39.

put down the thing as he meant it and let the meter limp along as best it could. For the idea was the inspiration, was it not? and the meter and rhyme were no more than the Understanding's method of decking out what the Reason had perceived in one of its great silences. They should not be abandoned, as Whitman abandoned them, because they were the conventional graces which established a community of feeling between the poet and the reader; but the moment that they asserted any claim of their own they became an offense and a hindrance. What Emerson does not seem to have laid to heart in this connection is that

> "Tasks in hours of insight willed
> May be through hours of gloom fulfilled."

Perhaps he did not dare tamper with what the spirit had said to him; perhaps he was more eager to supply new messages than to polish and correct the old ones; perhaps he had that fear of mere art, of "rhetoric," which all men of deep sincerity have shared. When, as in the little poem called "The Snow Storm," the thought is merely pretty and poetic the art is fully adequate; and in proportion as the thought is high the expression is (in general) inadequate. If Emerson had chosen to work over his poems as Tennyson worked over his, he might, perhaps, have been as fine a poet as Tennyson; but those who, as Matthew Arnold puts it, "would live in the spirit" would have missed something infinitely more precious.

BIBLIOGRAPHY

All of the material given in the standard Riverside Edition of Emerson's works is included, together with additional matter, in the Centenary Edition, edited with introductions and notes by Edward Waldo Emerson. Both these editions, as well as the Journals, are published by Houghton, Mifflin & Co. A later volume of "Uncollected Writings" was published by The Lamb Publishing Company (New York). Emerson's Correspondence with Carlyle, with Sterling, and with Grimm has also been published. Additional letters are given in Furness's "Records of a Lifelong Friendship." Besides these, there is Emerson's contribution to the Memoirs of Margaret Fuller Ossoli.

A full bibliography of Emerson by George Willis Cooke was published in 1908 (Houghton). The criticisms published since then may be found in the A. L. A. indices and publishers' catalogues, and it has seemed unnecessary to list them. With the exception of a few articles in some of the less known periodicals and newspapers, the writer has had access to all of these criticisms, and those which have seemed of especial value have in one way or another found mention in the text or footnotes. The Index of Names will therefore supply the place of a completer bibliography. A selected list of books and articles is given.

Alcott, Amos Bronson: Ralph Waldo Emerson: Philosopher and Seer. Boston: Cupples, Hurd, 1888.

Alexander, James Waddel: Review of Emerson's First Series of Essays in Princ. R. 13: 539. 1841.

American Review: "Emerson and Transcendentalism," 1:233. 1845.

Arnold, Matthew: Discourses in America. Macmillan, 1885.

Bartol, Cyrus A.: "Emerson's Religion" in Genius and Character of Emerson.

Bowen, Francis: Review of *Nature* in Christian Examiner 21:371. 1837.

Brann, Henry A.: "Hegel and his New England Echo" in Cath. W. 41:56. 1885.

Cabot, James Elliot: A Memoir of Ralph Waldo Emerson. Houghton, 1887.

Chapman, John Jay: Emerson and Other Essays. New York: Scribners, 1898.

Conway, Moncure Daniel: Emerson at Home and Abroad. Boston: Osgood, 1882.

Cooke, George Willis: Ralph Waldo Emerson: His Life, Writings, and Philosophy. Houghton, 1882.

Dewey, John: "The Philosopher of Democracy" in Internat. J. of Ethics, 13:405.

Dugard, M.: Ralph Waldo Emerson, Sa vie et son œuvre. Paris: Libraire Armand Colin, 1907.

Dutton, J. F.: "Emerson's Optimism" in Unitar. R. 35:127. 1891.

Eliot, Charles W.: "Emerson as Seer" in Atlan. Mo. 91:844. 1903.

Emerson, Edward Waldo: Emerson in Concord. Houghton, 1889.

Firkins, Oliver W.: Ralph Waldo Emerson. Houghton, 1914.

Francke, Kuno: "Emerson and German Personality" in German Ideals of To-day. Houghton, 1907.

Frothingham, Octavius Brooks: Transcendentalism in New England. New York: Putnams, 1876.

Garnett, Richard: Life of Emerson. Great Writers Series. London: Scott, 1888.

Genius and Character of Emerson, edited by Franklin B. Sanborn. Boston: Osgood, 1885. Contains notable essays by friends of Emerson in the Concord School of Philosophy.

Goddard, Harold Clarke: Studies in New England Transcendentalism. Columbia University doctoral dissertation. New York, 1908.

Guernsey, Alfred Hudson: Ralph Waldo Emerson: Philosopher and Poet. New York: Appletons, 1881.

Harris, William T.: "The Dialectic Unity in Emerson's Prose" in J. of Spec. Phil. 18:195. 1884. "Emerson's Philosophy of Nature" in Genius and Character of Emerson.

Haskins, David Greene: Ralph Waldo Emerson: His Maternal Ancestors, with some Reminiscences of him. Boston: Cupples, Upham, 1887.

Hecker, Isaac T.: "Two Prophets of this Age" in Cath. W. 47:684. 1888.

Hedge, Frederic Henry: Memorial address in J. H. Allen's Our Liberal Movement in Theology.

Holmes, Oliver Wendell: Ralph Waldo Emerson. American Men of Letters Series. Boston: Houghton, 1885.

Ireland, Alexander: Ralph Waldo Emerson: His Life, Genius, and Writings. London: Simpkin, Marshall, 1882.

James, William: Address on Emerson in Memories and Studies.

Lee, Vernon: "Emerson, Transcendentalist and Utilitarian," in Contemp. R. 67:345. 1895.

Literary World: Emerson Number, May 22, 1880, contains brief articles by Hedge, Bartol, Higginson, Walt Whitman, Curtis, Sanborn, Cooke, and others.

Mead, Edwin D.: The Influence of Emerson. Boston: A. U. A., 1903. "Emerson's Ethics" in Genius and Character of Emerson.

Milnes, Richard Monckton: "American Philosophy—Emerson's Works," in Westminster R. 33:345. 1840.

Morley, John: Ralph Waldo Emerson: An Essay. Macmillan, 1884. Also in Critical Miscellanies.

Nicoll, William R.: "Ralph Waldo Emerson." in North Amer. R. 176:675. 1903.

O'Connor, J. F. X.: "Ralph Waldo Emerson" in Cath. W. 27:90. 1878.

Orr, John: "Transcendentalism of New England" in Internat. R. 13:381. 1882.

Parker, Theodore: Lecture on Transcendentalism, Works, Centenary Edition, vol. VI.

Princeton R. 11:95 (1839) "Transcendentalism"; 13:539 (1841) "Pantheism."

Rands, William B.: "Transcendentalism in England, New England, and India" in Contemp. R. 29:469.

Riley, I. Woodbridge: American Thought. Holt, 1915.

Ripley, George: "Philosophic Thought in Boston" in Memorial History of Boston. Osgood, 1880.

Robertson, John M.: Modern Humanists. London: Swan Sonnenschein, 1891.

Roz, Firmin: "L'Idéalisme américain: Ralph Waldo Emerson," in Revue des deux mondes, 70:651. 1902.

Salter, William M.: "Emerson's Views of Society and Reform," in Internat. J. of Ethics 13:414. 1903.

Sanborn, Franklin Benjamin: The Personality of Emerson. Boston: Goodspeed, 1903.

Santayana, George: Interpretations of Poetry and Religion. Scribners, 1900.

Social Circle in Concord. Riverside Press, 1903. Contains addresses by LeBaron Russell Briggs, Samuel Hoar, Charles Eliot Norton, Thomas Wentworth Higginson, William James, and others.

Thayer, William Roscoe: The Influence of Emerson. Boston: Cupples, Upham, 1886.

Tiffany, Francis: "Transcendentalism: the New England Renaissance," in Unitar. R. 31:111.

Ward, Julius Hammond: "Emerson in New England Thought," in Andover R. 8:380. 1887.

Wendell, Barrett: A Literary History of America. Scribners, 1901.

Wilson, S. Law: The Theology of Modern Literature. Edinburgh: Clark, 1899.

Woodberry, George Edward: Ralph Waldo Emerson. New York: Macmillan, 1907. English Men of Letters Series.

Woodbury, Charles J.: Talks with Ralph Waldo Emerson. New York: Baker, Taylor.

INDEX